THE TYRANNY OF
POLITICAL
IGNORANCE

CRACKS IN THE UNITED STATES DEMOCRATIC ARMOR

WINSTON SHEEKEL MARSH

Archway Publishing books may be ordered through booksellers or by contacting:

Archway Publishing
1663 Liberty Drive
Bloomington, IN 47403
www.archwaypublishing.com
844-669-3957

ISBN: 978-1-4808-9898-1 (sc)
ISBN: 978-1-4808-9897-4 (hc)
ISBN: 978-1-4808-9899-8 (e)

Library of Congress Control Number: 2020922189

Print information available on the last page.

Archway Publishing rev. date: 11/13/2020

Contents

Acknowledgments

M any people encouraged me to write this book. They include all my high school students in American Government classes and former college students of Comparative Politics and International Relations. They have always insisted that my perspectives on national government and international relations should be put in writing. My baby brother, Glendon Marsh, who lives on New York, thinks my depth and breadth of political knowledge is remarkable. In all our telephone conversations, he has urged me to put my thoughts in writing. I have finally summed up the courage to take them up on their challenge.

This book would not have been possible without the help of my colleague and technology mentor, Dr. Tiffany West, who devoted countless hours to get my manuscript to meet publication standards. Her mastery of the technology field made it possible for all our communications, image searches and locations, and formatting and book design choices to be done remotely. Without this level of competence and willingness, the project would have been impossible with the coronavirus pandemic spiking in our locality.

My wife, Marvalyn, and daughter, Robyn, offered immeasurable support throughout the process and particularly in those times when it appeared that synchronization would not be possible for all the pieces of the project. They also permitted several facets of their lives to be put on hold until the conclusion of this endeavor, and for this, I owe them an eternal debt of gratitude.

1
INTRODUCTION

The events swirling around in the United States today conjure up images of destruction and doom. In all aspects of life, events appear to be out of line with what is known and expected of this mighty nation. The coronavirus pandemic is wreaking havoc, and there is this sickening feeling that the nation's leaders do not know what they are doing. The world is also in shock. Everybody everywhere thought the United States would be the country that took the lead in crushing this coronavirus disease. Shockingly, the United States is at the back of the line in the worldwide race to contain the coronavirus disease. The disease has already infected more than eight million Americans and killed more than 220, 000. There is no end in sight. Blacks and minorities are disproportionately affected by this strange and invisible disease, a natural outcome of the years of neglect engendered by systemic racism.

As if this was not enough, the brutal killing of George Floyd on the streets of Minneapolis created an explosion of marches all over the country as the Black Lives Matter movement spun into action, demanding justice. The marches exploded all over the world, even in countries where few or no blacks live. It appears that overnight the United States' leadership is smitten with paralysis. All around the country, one sees hunger, unemployment, homelessness, locked-down businesses, sickness, and death. Nothing seems to be going right. Students have been locked out of school for more than seven months. The infection and death rates are climbing at astronomical levels, but the government is insisting on opening up the schools, sending students, teachers, and support personnel to face the infection and death that are the hallmarks of this scourge. It is as if all the United States has gone mad. The back-to-school plan is bound to exacerbate the crisis.

Events like these are shocking, but with careful analysis, it becomes clear that they did not spring up overnight. They are usually the climax of a series of behaviors that have been deteriorating for decades and possibly for centuries. It is usually the outcome of developments that have been perpetuated under the pretense that they were the best for the country. The structure of the society creates an environment where some classes exploit others, creating a façade that the nation is progressing rapidly and is supposedly better than all other nations. In an effort to advance the free enterprise system, businesses carry out assaults on the environment and establish their hazardous industries in poor and minority communities. Citizens of these communities are highly susceptible to all manner of diseases. Blacks and minorities are usually the first victims of strange, new diseases such as the coronavirus.

Astonishingly, in the 2016 presidential election, the politically ignorant electorate elected Donald J. Trump as president of the United States. President Trump is arguably the most politically ignorant individual ever to gain ascendency to that high office. On his political campaign, he planned to reverse all the environmental regulations imposed by his predecessor. He kept his promise to a great extent, thereby exacerbating the horrible conditions under which some poor communities are forced to live. The coronavirus pandemic zoomed in on these communities with laser focus.

The coronavirus pandemic is an exposer of truth, and the killing of George Floyd is the straw that broke the camel's back. Future generations may observe these two cataclysmic events as a blessing because they will engender a reexamination of the United States' political, economic, and social direction and help to bring about a truly equitable society. In a sense the election of the most politically ignorant individual as president may also turn out to be a blessing because nothing has highlighted more efficiently the imbalances that have been perpetuated in this country for centuries.

In the pages that follow, an attempt will be made to examine the United States' history from colonial days through its independence to the present times. It is hoped that at the end of these pages, some of the flaws in the development of the United States will be exposed. More importantly, it is hoped that the United States' leadership will have the courage to return to the drawing board and address the inequalities that have prevented many Americans from achieving the equality goals embedded in the Declaration of Independence. In the process, they will also ensure that the equal protection clause of the Fourteenth Amendment becomes a reality for all American peoples.

It is also hoped that the United States Congress and the states will take the necessary steps to amend the Constitution to modify the qualifications for future presidents. The president and congresspersons should have to pass an approved examination and demonstrate competence in prescribed requirements to qualify to hold office in the United States government. The electorate should also be exposed to a revivalist political training program to ensure a more knowledgeable electorate. These developments will ensure that neither the future electorate nor future presidents will ever again display the level of political ignorance that got Donald Trump elected to the highest office in the United States. These proposed developments will promote the engagement of all Americans in the political process. They will also ensure that the tyranny of political ignorance never again rears its ugly head in the United States of America.

2
EARLY DEVELOPMENTS

C racks in the United States' democratic armor have been an ever-present phenomenon. The framers of the United Sates Constitution ran into difficulties with the equality pronouncements in the Declaration of Independence at the Constitutional Convention in Philadelphia in 1787. The presence of a slave population, mostly in the southern states, created tension between the northern non-slave states and the southern slave-owning ones over the equality issue. A few of the delegates at the Constitutional Convention in 1787 wanted to put an end to slavery, but their protests were drowned out by the white supremacist southern slave owners. Hence the United States' democratic armor was constructed with a known defect—systemic racism. This defect was a major flaw, a carryover from the colonial days.

The 167 years prior to the draft of the United States Constitution was essentially the history of white supremacist control over slavery, which came to dominate colonial life and was ultimately encoded in the seminal documents of the United States of America. The United States Constitution legalized slavery in 1787, creating a flawed democratic armor. The process of dehumanizing the African slaves and stripping them of all human dignity was well advanced. The Virginia House of Burgesses was the initiator of the dehumanizing process, but all the slave-owning states later adapted the Virginia slave-control template. Even those states that depended on paid labor to drive their economies were affected by the institution of slavery. Blacks in non-slave states were not treated much differently from those in slave states. Freed blacks were heavily restricted by the colonial/states' vagrancy laws. Institutional racism was a contagious disease from the conception of the United States. It became the center of gravity in the early United States democracy around which other flaws gravitated and swirled, creating a political, economic, and social vortex. Domestic and foreign developments exerted pressure on the United States to reexamine its production methodologies as the Industrial Revolution spread across the world in the early nineteenth century. A wave of Enlightenment thinking also played a significant role in the demand for change. As a result of the southern United States' resistance to change, the political, economic, and social vortex spun out of control in 1861 and exploded in the Civil War between the Northern and Southern states. Hostilities simmered down with the emancipation of the slaves and a victory for the Union forces, but systemic racism has a natural proclivity to regenerate itself and to work toward other social unrests and explosions.

Currently, the most gaping crack in the United States' democratic armor shows up in the form of political ignorance. Political ignorance is used here to mean that the electorate is not using the available information to guide voting decisions. Because the individual vote is regarded as a negligible variable in election outcomes, individuals should use available information to make voting a societal obligation. This means the electorate should be voting to determine the advantages of their vote to the society as a whole and not so much for the individual's benefits.

Russell Neuman and fellow researchers observed the growing political ignorance of the American electorate and documented this decline over the four decades between 1948 and 1980. In *The Paradox of Mass Politics,* Neuman claims that the United States' political process appears to work well, in spite of the pervasive political ignorance of the electorate. Year after year, the electorate appears to make the right decisions at the polls, giving the impression that political ignorance is not a threat to the United States' democracy. However, in the presidential election of 2016, a foreign adversarial state actor attempted to disrupt the relatively smooth flow of the United States' democratic institutions by exploiting this ignorance.

This foreign state actor has long been looking at the findings of Russell Neuman's *The Paradox of Mass Politics*, in which he propounded the theory that the United States' electorate is fundamentally politically ignorant and mostly unsophisticated. It was considered a marvel that the system worked as well as it did, given this level of political ignorance. Furthermore, it was obvious then that the United States had been playing Russian roulette (pun intended) with its political processes. In the 2016 presidential election, social media, where anything and everything goes, quickly became the Russian playground to engage and exploit the United States' political ignorance.

To add to this drama, probably the most politically ignorant candidate ever to run for the United States presidency in the person of Donald J. Trump emerged as the candidate for one of the major political parties. This emboldened the foreign state actor to step up its effort to exploit this obvious crack in the United States' democratic armor. Russia, the United States' most dangerous geopolitical adversary, had a self-proclaimed friend in Donald J. Trump, the Republican candidate who inexplicably insisted on having a great relationship with the Russian president, Vladimir Putin.

Adherents of international relations saw this as a cat-and-mouse relationship. They saw Putin as the cat, the former seasoned intelligence operative and head of the KBG (Committee of State Security) seeking to restore Russia's former superpower glory. They saw Trump as the mouse, this politically ignorant player, unable to use historical hindsight to make informed judgment, yet willing to engage this adversarial player whose priority is to weaken the United States, the world's only standing superpower.

The Federal Bureau of Investigation and the Central Intelligence Agency picked up on the foreign state actor's attempt to interfere in the United States' political process, but the sitting president, Barack Obama, hesitated to disrupt this attempt and inform the American electorate for fear of appearing partisan and aiding the more anti-Russian candidate, Hillary Clinton, in the presidential election contest. President Obama, like many other Americans up to this stage of the campaign, did not give candidate Donald J. Trump a chance of winning the 2016 presidential election. History may yet prove this to be a regrettable miscalculation. This moment of vacillation probably opened the door for political ignorance to tyrannize the American society.

Republican candidate Donald J. Trump is not insane (mad) in the conventional sense of the term. He is not a genius in the conventional sense of the term either. What is true though is that he is an insane genius. He may take umbrage with the *insane* label, but he has already branded himself a genius, although his meaning of the term may not match the cynicism implied here. His political campaign and his victory in the 2016 presidential election confirmed this assessment. Americans who observed previous political campaigns did not give him many chances of winning the 2016 election. Most of what he said and did during the 2016 presidential campaign would have resulted in an ignominious defeat for any other previously known candidate.

Candidate Trump began his campaign by attacking what all Americans accept as a given, an irrefutable fact, that the United Sates is a nation of immigrants. The insane genius descended the elevator at the Trump Tower and launched his presidential campaign by attacking Mexican immigrants as murderers, rapists, and drug addicts.

The president's strategy to secure the United States / Mexican border and
prevent undocumented foreigners from coming into the United States

Candidate Trump planned to build a wall to shut the immigrants
out, and Mexico, he claimed, would pay for the wall. Later on in his
campaign, he wanted all Muslims banned until he knew "what the
hell is going on." In subsequent months, candidate Trump began the
process of insulting other immigrant families. He pledged to deport
the estimated twelve million undocumented immigrants living in the
United States when he became president, all this while playing to his
political base.

When candidate Trump made disparaging statements about a fallen
army captain and remarked that he and his family should never have
been able to serve in the United States Armed Services, he incensed

a lot of military families all over the country, but that did not deter the insane genius, candidate Trump, one bit. The father of the fallen army captain thought candidate Trump was most ignorant about the United States Constitution. He pulled out a copy of the Constitution from his pocket and offered to lend it to candidate Trump. He had no idea that candidate Trump had a reading problem. He does not like to read. Trump was unperturbed and continued his attack on immigrant families throughout the campaign.

At one of his campaign rallies, candidate Trump referred to an African American gentleman as "My African American," putting his ignorance about systemic racism on display. During slavery, African Americans were property of white supremacist owners, mainly in the South. African Americans will eternally disdain any suggestion of belonging to anyone. Early in his administration, President Donald J. Trump explained that he would prefer immigrants coming in from Norway instead of from s***hole countries. Insane! His latest move against immigrants is to curtail the number of H-1B visas that high technology firms can request. This decision is currently negatively affecting the recruitment of foreign medical personnel to combat the coronavirus pandemic. The president made that decision guided by the fallacious assumption that the United States no longer needs immigrants. This is also part of a strategy to promote a nationalist agenda. Some believe this is part of President's Trump's desire—to make America white again.

A careful examination of candidate Trump's political platform, "To Make America Great Again," would show that it was on a pathway to failure from its beginnings. To build a campaign that goes after immigrants is to begin to tear down the fabric of the United States. The United States without immigrants is naked and exposed. At every turn of its development, the United States has had to bring immigrants into the country to satisfy its labor needs. This includes the slavery issue. The United States still brings in an estimated one million immigrants annually. Moreover, at a time when most developed countries are looking at the possibility of chronic labor shortages as their populations aged, the United States is supremely positioned to preempt this eventuality by increasing its annual intake of immigrants. If candidate Trump was a visionary leader, he would have picked up on this trend and begun to prepare to address the estimated twelve million undocumented aliens already living in the country. The majority of these undocumented aliens are hardworking, enterprising people, simply looking for a better standard of living than the one they left behind as they fled their countries of origin. An amnesty and a pathway to citizenship seem the logical policies to implement if a United States president wants to make American great again.

In the 2016 election, however, the American electorate was exposed to the most degrading levels of political adversarial behavior. The current president of the United States, Donald J. Trump, rose to the office by publicly destroying the character of his fellow Republican rivals during the 2016 presidential campaign. These were an agglomeration of illustrious people, former and current governors of states, senators of the United States government, successful members of corporate society, and a prominent neurosurgeon. Feeding on the electorate's lack of political sophistication, presidential candidate Donald J. Trump disrespected the office by using the vilest language and the most demeaning terms to put down his opponents. He threatened violence and offered to pay the court costs of those who assaulted dissenters at his political gatherings.

After he demolished his Republican rivals, Donald J. Trump turned on his Democratic counterpart, a former friend, and described her as "Crooked Hillary" and chanted "Lock her up" during and after the campaign up to the present moment. This is a woman who is very highly educated and was First Lady in the state of Arkansas twice, as her husband, Bill Clinton, served as governor. She was First Lady of the United States when her husband served two terms as president. Hillary Clinton was senator of New York for two terms and Secretary of State under President Barack Obama, who defeated her in the presidential primary of 2008, when civility was still alive. Hillary Clinton is a highly respected woman nationally and internationally. Donald Trump trampled on her dignity and murdered American civility during the 2016 campaign.

One thing must be said about Donald J. Trump, the presidential candidate: he did not hide his mean spirit, his vulgar approach to civility, his wanton disregard for women and minorities, and his disdain for the truth; nor did he hide his sexual predatory practices. He, however, hid his tax obligations, which may conceal some very shady deals.

What is amazing is that this dastardly behavior powered Donald J. Trump to the highest office in the United States and in the world. The question must be asked, Is this the death of Russell Neuman's *paradox of mass politics,* the idea that the American political process seems to work fairly well in spite of the apparent political ignorance of the electorate? Or is this an indictment on the American people who voted Donald J. Trump into the White House, rewarding him for his outrageous behavior during the 2016 presidential campaign?

The truth is that the politically knowledgeable minority knew that it must elect a president on merit and not on popularity. At the state level, the mass of the American electorate put their political ignorance on display and voted for Donald J. Trump, in spite of the predictable downward spiral of American dreams and aspirations. The politically ignorant ignored the call of the fifty Republican Party officials who warned that Donald Trump was not ethically, morally, or intellectually fit to hold the office. Some Americans had to see all of the insane genius's destructive qualities and shortcomings as a leader before they would believe that this very successful businessman is really not fit for the office.

Many Americans basked in the glory of President Trump's victory in 2016 without a thought of the repercussions. Technological advancements have made the world a village. The United States' neighbors are looking on in horror. Right before their eyes; the great hegemon, the United States of America, has crumbled into a repugnant, vile, and ugly mass. The leaders of Saudi Arabia welcomed President Trump with open arms, claiming that they have no interest in the domestic politics that got him elected; they just want to make deals with the new president of the United States. The French leader uttered similar words. Both leaders tacitly admitted that they are more interested in economic deals regardless of the moral and ethical costs.

President Trump's firing of the FBI director James Comey engendered the establishment of a special counsel by the acting attorney general, Rosenstein, to oversee the investigation of the alleged Russian interference in the 2016 presidential election. This decision had various repercussions. For example, the newly appointed attorney general, Jeff Sessions, who was candidate Trump's close adviser during the presidential campaign, realized that there would be conflict of interest and immediately recused himself in the handling of the investigation of Russia's interference in the 2016 presidential election. President Trump's fury was palpable, and so was his political ignorance regarding the image and functions of the attorney general.

When President Trump, the politically ignorant leader of the free world, first appeared among representatives of the foreign adversarial power in a White House meeting, he seemed submissive and apologetic to his Russian overlords.

President Donald J. Trump meeting with the Russian ambassador
in the White House, excluding the American press

One got the impression that the bosses were angry with the underling, President Trump, for his slow pace in returning favors. The underling quickly explained that the FBI director's probe was a burden around his neck. Now that he had shaken that off, he was in a better position to do the master's bidding.

In the future, he would do all in his power to remove existing sanctions against the Russians and stave off the United States Congress's future attempts to impose new ones. It should be observed that the American people knew all this only because it was beamed on Russian television. President Trump had barred the United States press from this meeting in the people's house. This is further proof that President Donald Trump has a very low regard for the American people's right to know what is going on in his administration.

To its credit, however, the United States Congress demonstrated a little bit of spunk; it used its override authority to put President Trump in a very awkward situation. President Trump had the option to sign the imposition of the new sanctions on the foreign adversarial interloper or face the embarrassment of a congressional override, even though his party controlled both houses of Congress. However, partisan politics limited Congress's power to address the problem in a more comprehensive manner.

President Trump's political ignorance manifests itself in the many ways he tramples on constitutional norms and the government's standing operating procedures. For example, President Trump has not followed the law and filled vacancies in critical administrative departments when they occur. By filling vacancies with acting personnel, he creates instability in these departments. The president's failure to fill vacancies could, in emergency situations, result in critical delays in responding to crises, as evidenced by the time lost in moving meaningfully against the coronavirus pandemic.

Even more importantly, it appears that filling these vacancies with acting personnel is a calculated ploy to give President Trump more flexibility. Given the president's admiration for dictators and the way they carry out policies, failure to fill vacancies could signal that this president is inclined to disrupt the democratic process in the United States for sinister purposes. For the first time in the nation's history, questions are being raised about a smooth transition of power in the event that President Trump loses at the polls in 2020. The electorate should not forget that candidate Trump remarked in the 2016 campaign that there would be a civil war if he lost. The White House staff claimed he was being humorous. However, in a recent interview with Fox News network, President Trump could not commit to a smooth transition of power if he loses in the 2020 presidential election. This is evidence that he has no intention to yield power. The United States' transition to autocratic rule is not as far-fetched as it was in the pre-Trump era.

What is even more threatening to the United States' democracy is that these acting officials have not passed through the scrutiny of the United States Senate in the checks and balances principles of the Constitution. Erosion of the Constitution could start with small trickles like hiring personnel without senatorial vetting. The excessive number of acting personnel in the Trump administration poses additional risks in crises situations. This could be catastrophic immediately after a transition of power. The new president could be greatly incapacitated by not having departments that are staffed with the best experts who are capable of demonstrating high-level competencies in standard operating procedures. This could be the difference between success or failure, victory or defeat, at the national and international levels of operation.

Coupled with the lack of respect for the office of the presidency is Donald Trump's unadulterated bigotry. The world respected and honored the ideals of the United States for centuries and has watched the struggle to make equality a reality, sluggish though these steps may be. When Barack Obama ran for and won the presidency of the United States, it appeared that its leadership of the free world would continue without question. This, it seemed, was a nation that respected the rights of all peoples, both at home and abroad. People around the world felt that with the United States as leader of the free world, their sons and daughters could dream of changes and aspire to lead at the highest levels.

This is not to say that all Americans welcomed the ascendency of Barack Obama to the presidency. The United States' democratic system is an adversarial one. It is understood that the majority voted for Barack Obama, but a sizeable minority, including Donald J. Trump and his white supremacist associates, did not. This is how the system has functioned for more than 230 years.

President Donald J. Trump has demeaned every institution that the United States holds dear. He has attacked every relationship with foreign powers that took decades to put together, relationships that have held the world in relative peace for more than seventy years and prevented a third world war or—worse—a nuclear one. These relationships were carefully crafted by the world's most admired statesmen and stateswomen. The United Nations, the North Atlantic Treaty Organization, the North American Free Trade Agreement, the Paris Agreement (climate change), and the Trans Pacific Partnership are all under attack. This leads one to ask, Is Donald J. Trump a de facto Russian agent? Vladimir Putin regards most of these relationships as a stumbling block to Russia's territorial aggrandizement and superpower aspirations.

Objective thinkers do not have a problem with Donald J. Trump's challenge to these international agreements and the asymmetrical nature of some of them. Nothing is wrong in observing that some participants are not meeting their full financial obligations in the defense costs for the region in which they live. Nor is it wrong to point out the anomalies and shortcomings in bilateral contracts. What is wrong is the tone and the adversarial approach to nations the United States has regarded as friends and allies for almost a century. Changes are always welcomed, but the strategies used to initiate change can be distasteful. It must also be remembered that most of these nations sided with the United States in pushing back Iraq's attempt to disrupt the West's oil supply by grabbing Kuwait in 1991. They also demonstrated solidarity with the United States in the aftermath of the bombing of the World Trade Center and the subsequent war with Afghanistan. If Donald J. Trump wins a second term as president, the reparation of relationships with these allies will be delayed and may worsen precipitously. Whoever succeeds Donald J. Trump will have to devote a great deal of time to mending fences and trust in the United States leadership. Many believe that trust lost can never be regained. Cynics believe there will be nothing after President Donald J. Trump.

3

TEARING DOWN OBAMA'S LEGACY

W ell-intentioned aspirants to the United States presidency dream of standing on the shoulders of the giants who served before them and hope that they will be able to initiate a few changes of their own as they learn to manage the awesome responsibilities entrusted to them. Most come with open minds and surround themselves with qualified individuals who they hope will guide them away from pitfalls. First-time presidents are usually nervous and do their best to avoid early missteps. Most have been humble yet assertive when issues relate to the people's interest. Some try early in their careers to make a statement that will become the catchphrase for their presidency. President John F. Kennedy's stands out, "Ask not what your country can do for you; ask what you can do for your country." This simple statement signals that it would be the people's interest first and not that of the president.

Donald J. Trump, on the other hand, entered the White House with President Obama foremost on his mind. His first effort was rather petty. President Trump made a great effort to demonstrate that he, Donald J. Trump, had a larger inauguration crowd than his predecessor. The pettiness emerged on day one of his presidency. A comparison of pictures taken of the two inaugurations clearly showed that Obama's inauguration was the larger of the two. The Trump administration lied and stuck to the lie in the face of open criticism. This has become a feature of the Trump administration. The nation is bombarded with lies on a daily basis. It shows disrespect for the American people and spreads a great deal of confusion. What is even more alarming is that President Trump's political base believes the lies. It is also a feature of the tyranny of political ignorance.

The genius in Donald J. Trump led him to attack all of President Barack Obama's regulatory practices, no matter that they were initiated for the public good. For example, moving away from coal to solar and other sustainable forms of energy saved lives and brought about improved standards of living, but Donald J. Trump promised the people in the coal-mining districts to bring back coal. "Clean coal, beautiful coal" became a constant refrain during the 2016 presidential campaign. From a practical point of view, jobs seemed more important to the unemployed population than the environmental damage, ill health, and possible death that come with increased coal mining.

Ironically, Donald J. Trump inherited an economy that was on the uptick in employment. This trend gained momentum under the Trump administration, but the employment uptick had very little to do with clean-coal processing, as Candidate Trump touted during his campaign. The clean-coal promotion won him many votes though. Currently, the Trump administration is no longer focusing on coal. Natural gas and other forms of sustainable energy are taking precedent over clean coal.

Prior to the start of the 2016 campaign, Donald J. Trump read the discontent in the nation very well. The period when the Tea Party held sway in American politics gave him a lot of ideas. It was white supremacists' disaffection with a black President Obama in the White House that gave rise to Donald Trump's conspiracy theories. The birther movement was the test case for this nefarious concept. It involves playing upon the ignorance of the electorate. Tell a blatant lie that is frighteningly alarming, and the politically ignorant electorate will not bother to use available information to challenge the lie. Many of them will believe the lie at face value because of who is projecting it.

The idea that President Barack Obama was not born on United Sates soil and therefore did not qualify to be the president is plain nonsense when it is checked out against available information. However, citizen

Trump, the genius, knew that most Americans would refute this absurdity, but his white supremacist associates would latch on to it. Yes, the birther movement created a base, small though it might have been. However, it is worth noting that more than 50 percent of Republicans today still believe that President Obama was not born in the United States. Ignorance dominates. Some believe President Obama was born in Hawaii but still argue that he was not born in the United States.

The conspiracy theories have multiplied exponentially since Donald Trump assumed the presidency. They include the idea that massive election fraud denied him the popular vote in the 2016 national election count. President Trump, in the face of the facts to the contrary, still holds the position that his victory in the 2016 presidential election involved a majority in the Electoral College as well as in the popular vote. Even though the Federal Bureau of Investigation's chief can find no evidence to support the idea that the Obama administration spied on the Trump campaign, President Trump continues to insist that it happened. The conspiracy theories extend into the media-reporting domain. President Trump extols the nation not to believe what they see and hear. Anything that does not work in President Trump's favor is branded as "fake news," and no matter how evident the truth is, the Trump administration claims that it has "alternative facts" to refute what is published. The most recent case involving alternative facts is the reality that the United States has one of the highest coronavirus death rates among developed economies. President Trump, in the Fox News interview, called on his aides to bring him details to the contrary.

Moreover, as globalism and the concept of comparative advantage gripped the world and started to shift manufacturing output to populations that were better educated, more disciplined, and less expensive, Donald Trump and likeminded xenophobes placed the blame on the incumbent Obama administration. Outsourcing production to other countries became a survival methodology for many United States manufacturers who had to survive in a viciously competitive free enterprise environment. As people in the rust belt complained about outsourcing and their diminishing standards of living, Donald J. Trump saw an opportunity to exploit this development to his advantage. The promises he made to this population to bring back the jobs significantly grew his base. Local manufacturing has gained some momentum in the United States since President Trump assumed the office of the presidency, but experts credit most of this increase to market forces and not to President Trump's initiatives. His base praises him for the gains though.

The Affordable Care Act holds out the prospects of becoming America's most far-reaching legislative initiative in the twenty-first century, and this grates at the nerves of President Trump, the apparent racist who envies the ascendency of all black people. That the Affordable Care Act appears to be a shining legacy for President Obama is anathema to President Donald Trump. That a black man should assume the United States presidency is maddening by itself. To be the president who successfully established a national health care plan, a hundred years after it was first conceptualized by President Teddy Roosevelt, is too much for President Trump to bear.

President Trump does not want to kill the Affordable Care Act because it is bad. He plots its demise because it is too good to be credited to a black president. President Trump is so incensed by a black person holding the office of the presidency that he wants to destroy everything that Barack Obama achieved as president. The Model T Ford was not perfect when it was invented. It was not unceremoniously discarded though. Over the years, all the flaws were fixed. Today, the nation has a near-perfect machine. The first airplane was not discarded either. Improvements have brought it to near perfection. So the "Obamacare invention," if given time and effort, will blossom out to become a centerpiece of the American dream. That is President Trump's greatest fear.

Bringing Iran to the conference table seemed like an impossible task until Barack Obama, as a candidate for the presidency and as president of the United States, insisted that it must happen. Statesmen and stateswomen of five great powers of the world, plus Germany, got together with the urging of President Obama and hammered out a deal called the Joint Comprehensive Plan of Action (JCPA). Under the JCPA, Iran agreed to forgo its nuclear ambition in exchange for the lifting of sanctions imposed on it by the international community. Many visionary leaders regard a nuclear Iran as an unpredictable variable in international security.

Deals are never intended to change a nation's ideology and values, nor are they intended to bring about regime change. They are target specific. In the case of Iran, the target was to get that country to abandon its nuclear ambition. It was not intended to be a deal imposed on Iran. It was a negotiated deal. Both sides had to give up something to get most of what they wanted. Donald Trump, the United States president, hates the Iran deal because, as he claims, the deal was one-sided. However, the president's previous behavior pattern leads observers to conclude that it was not because the deal failed to achieve the objectives of the negotiating powers but because the architect was Barack Obama. President Trump cannot allow a black man to have such an outstanding legacy. Therefore, the deal had to be dismantled.

President Trump planned to disrupt the Iran deal even though the signing powers found no violations by Iran. His strategy was to spread some confusion and hope that the entire deal would collapse. He gave no thought to the consequences of a nuclear Iran, so long as Barack Obama did not get credit for this unique accomplishment beside his name. It is rumored that Kim Jung Un has doubled his nuclear arsenal in response to President Trump's wishy-washy diplomacy. Iran is also back in the business of preparing centrifuges for bomb-making purposes. President Trump, through his behavior, has made himself a threat to national and international security.

In his desire to tear down the Obama legacy, President Trump sees the Paris Climate Agreement as making Barack Obama a giant president with monumental achievements, while Trump appears the dwarf who achieves nothing. The possibility that the climate change effort may work and begin to reverse global warming and give the praise to Barack Obama creates nightmares for President Trump. He withdraws the United Sates from the Paris Climate Agreement simply to rob President Obama of the recognition this would confer on him. The Trans Pacific Partnership keeps the United States current as the world's leader in trade and economic expansion, but because it was Barack Obama's initiative, it too had to go.

It would be simple common sense if one president builds on his predecessor's achievements while adding his own initiatives. To destroy all your predecessor's edifices to construct your own leaves you little time to get policies implemented. To date, all that President Trump has done is to destroy Barack Obama's policies. In reversing the Obama environmental regulations, President Trump may have inadvertently contributed to the outbreak of the coronavirus pandemic. Scientists believe that the disruption of the ecosystem makes it possible for wildlife to intermingle with human habitations and creates the possibility for viruses to jump from one species to another. That would be great irony, for the coronavirus pandemic is wreaking havoc with the economy that President Trump claims as his own, "the greatest economy" in the world.

4

TRAMPLING THE CONSTITUTION

C hecks and balances form one of the bedrock principles of the United States' democracy. Under the principle of checks and balances, the power to oversee the executive branch falls under the purview of the House of Representatives. The House of Representatives also has the sole power to bring impeachment charges against a sitting president of the United States. President Trump is not the first president to make the House of Representatives' ability to request executive files and documents difficult, but he is undoubtedly the president who has shown unparalleled disdain for this checks and balances function of the United States Congress.

Moreover, President Trump has blocked his aides from testifying before the House of Representatives and refused to turn over documents that could help the House to determine if the President, by his actions, is obstructing justice or violating the Constitution. President Trump has publicly displayed annoyance with the step-by-step procedures of the court system and with the checks and balances process. The President's behavior in this regard displays a wanton disregard for the public's right to know what is going on in his administration and in the United States. The House of Representatives is one of the main victims of the tyranny of political ignorance.

At the very beginning of his presidency, several of President Trump's ill-prepared executive orders were reversed by the courts. He lambasted one judge and referred to him as a so-called judge. Now, he is almost at the end of his first term and still has not come to grips with this issue. In a very recent decision regarding President Trump's request to overturn the Differed Action for Childhood Arrivals (DACA), the Supreme Court ruled against the president because his request did not follow administrative procedural law. In many instances, President Trump displayed ignorance about the legal process even though he promised to surround himself with the brightest and the best.

Both as candidate and president, Donald J. Trump broke and trampled on political norms. For example, most presidents of the United States took all the necessary precautions to make sure they were not violating the Constitution's emolument clause. Donald J. Trump the genius, however, during one of his early campaign events, signaled to the nation that he would be promoting his personal interests as president when he announced that his new hotel on Pennsylvania Avenue, not far from the White House, would soon be doing great business. Additionally, all presidential candidates since the 1970s have submitted their tax returns for public scrutiny. Candidate Trump did not, and as president, he has done all in his power to prevent Congress from getting access to his tax returns to determine if he is abusing his power. The Supreme Court very recently ruled that President Trump does not have absolute immunity against investigation while he is in office and that he will have to turn over his bank records to the prosecutor in the Southern District of New York, which is investigating the president for wrongdoing.

President Trump's display of intemperance with the courts and with checks and balances forms a crack in the Constitution's democratic armor because the weakening of these systems or their removal opens up the country to autocratic rule. This is a serious issue because President Trump has shown an un-American fascination with known dictators. For example, he is quite an admirer of Kim Jung Un, the North Korean dictator. He has expressed envy of this dictator's youth and the way he manages his country with the use of military force.

Moreover, President Trump has this absolute fascination with Vladimir Putin, the Russian leader. He is bent on forging a friendly relationship with Putin even though this leader has violated international law by his incursion in Ukraine. Putin violated Ukraine's sovereignty by grabbing Crimea and promoting separatist movements in the eastern part of that country. Ukraine is an ally of the United States, but President Trump was willing to withhold aid to this nation until its president agreed to carry out an investigation into the dealings of an American businessman, who happened to be the son of President Trump's potential rival in the 2020 presidential election.

It is interesting to note that President Donald J. Trump has never called out the Russians on their expansionist grabs. In fact, Donald J. Trump, the presidential candidate, claimed that the Russian never grabbed Crimea. The Russians probably do not believe they did either. Donald J. Trump is no prophet, yet during the presidential campaign of 2016, he predicted that the Russian hackers would track down Hilary Clinton's deleted emails. To those who are analytical thinkers, Donald Trump knew what the Russians were doing, and his utterance was more a slipup than a prophecy. Moreover, at the Helsinki Conference, President Trump betrayed his own intelligence personnel and took Vladimir Putin's word over that of his own intelligence experts. This poses a very serious question. What hold does Vladimir Putin have over the United States' president, Donald J. Trump?

Moreover, this betrayal exposes another crack in the United States' democratic armor. The founding fathers were very clear in emphasizing the dangers of foreign interference in the United States' domestic affairs. So egregious was President Trump's behavior that the House of Representatives, which had long resisted calls to impeach him, was compelled to act. This crack in the democratic armor appears to widen as members of the president's party turned a blind eye to all the emerging evidence or sought to rationalize them. House Republicans argued that it is the president's prerogative to conduct foreign affairs. This, they argued, made his request to the Ukrainian president to investigate a political rival part of his duties. If President Trump was ignorant about the consequences of withholding military support and funding to the Ukrainian allies, that does not make him guilty of a crime. Suddenly, President Trump's call on a foreign power to become involved in the United States' domestics affairs was seen as a norm by House Republicans. The House of Representatives invoked its power to impeach the president and charged him with two counts: abuse of power and obstruction of Congress to aid his own reelection.

In the event of an impeachment, the United States Senate, whose members are older and more matured, is entrusted with the responsibility of impartially reviewing the evidence and determining the president's guilt or innocence. In order to carry out this duty, the Senate is transformed into a court of law, with the Chief Justice of the United States Supreme Court presiding. The one hundred senators become the jurors in the impeachment trial. A new crack in the democratic armor appeared when the Senate majority leader publicly announced that he could not be impartial and that the Senate would not be impartial in examining the evidence against President Trump.

Exonerating President Donald J. Trump then, in his impeachment trial, was a foregone conclusion. The Senate wanted to exonerate the president without calling witnesses. President Trump was exonerated by the Senate's design. What is dangerous in these proceedings was that the United States Constitution was trampled on. School teachers and college and university professors groaned when this happened, for they teach by the book and the spirit of the Constitution and could not in their wildest dreams expect to hear senior Senate leaders publicly announce that they would not be impartial in the president's impeachment trial. Most Americans were shocked. What is even more alarming is that the nation is currently calling on the Senate to pass laws to encourage police officers to be impartial as they apprehend blacks and other minorities. The United States' 231-year-old political, social, and economic experiment is in serious jeopardy of failing on all fronts under the Trump administration.

Since his exoneration in the impeachment trial, President Trump has gone berserk. He fired all the witnesses who came forward in the impeachment trial and gave evidence of the president's inappropriate behaviors in trampling the rule of law. He has fired all the inspectors general who were investigating his wrongdoings. President Trump has intervened in court trials in order to get the prosecutors to drop cases or be lenient to his friends and close associates. He has extended presidential pardon to friends and associates who blatantly violated the law and received prison sentences. The president does have the right to pardon, but it is suspicious and distasteful when the pardons are directed at friends and associates. It may even be criminal.

House and Senate Republicans must share the blame for President Trump's behavior. They all behaved like wimps and abdicated their override and oversight powers and allowed the president to run amok. They have forgotten that the branches of government are coequal. This has allowed President Trump to demand 100 percent loyalty from them and threatens to destroy their political careers if they try to go against him in any way.

The framers expected the other two branches of government to check the power of the president when he appears to be out of control. Since President Trump was exonerated in his impeachment trial for abuse of power and obstruction of Congress for his personal gains, he has gone on to commit the very acts for which he was impeached. He continues to ask foreign countries for aid in defeating his opponent in the upcoming election, and he also continues to refuse to allow his aides to testify before Congress or to submit his income tax returns for review.

Congress's most egregious problem currently is partisan politics. The politics in the United States at the present moment could not be more polarized. President Donald J. Trump has made no attempt to unite the nation or to bridge the partisan divide. Instead, he stokes the divisive flames to his advantage. Until the House of Representatives and the Senate wake up and take their constitutional responsibilities seriously, President Trump will continue to abuse his powers and get away with it.

President Trump regards the courts as a stumbling block in his effort to impose his will on the American people. Do not disregard President Trump's projection of himself first in all his presidential dealings. Observe his fascination with Kim Jung Un, the North Korean president, Vladimir Putin of Russia, and Recep Tayyip Erdogan of Turkey. These are all dictators. Putin and Erdogan have manipulated their "democracies" so that they can remain in power for protracted periods beyond what their constitutions mandate. Trump's criticisms of the electoral process and how corrupt it is are setting the stage for this very eventuality should he win a second term.

The tyranny of political ignorance, explicit in a political campaign whose leader never misses a moment to speak glowingly of a geopolitical archrival, should have motivated Congress to recapture the founding fathers' fear of foreign interference in the nation's domestic politics. In this threat, Congress had an opportunity to fix the glaring anomalies in the system and prepare the United States to meet the challenges of comparative advantage, the burgeoning forces of demographic diversity, globalization, and the exploding scientific and technological advancements. Moreover, the United States Congress and the states are entrusted with the task of amending the Constitution. It is imperative that the Constitution be amended immediately to prevent a politically ignorant individual from ever assuming the presidency of the United States again.

Congress should begin to fix the problem, starting at the top. It is incumbent on Congress to examine the current constitutional qualifications for the presidency and declare it to be patently inadequate and dangerous for these times. As it stands, any rich, politically ignorant individual, born on United States soil and thirty-five years old or older, can assume the presidency of the United States. This actually happened in the presidential election of 2016 when Donald J. Trump assumed the office.

In fixing this shortcoming, Congress must simply establish a set of criteria that categorically state what future presidents should know, understand, and be able to do politically, both domestically and internationally, in order to enter the White House and learn the art of governing the nation and managing international diplomacy. To address this problem, Congress must challenge the leading academic institutions to put a curriculum together. The public should have an opportunity to critique this curriculum and make recommendations. A bipartisan committee of Congress must then review and approve this curriculum. Academia must be allowed to administer an examination that all future presidents and congresspersons must successfully complete to hold office in this democracy. It must be remembered that many congresspersons aspire to become president. Moreover, Congress must use its oversight powers to ensure that this addendum is meticulously observed.

The first United States president, George Washington, presided over a population of four million. Then there were thirteen states. Today there is a population of more than 330 million. There are now fifty states and the territories. The qualification for the presidency has not been changed over the past 233 years. The United States, in 1789, was basically an agriculturally based economy. The country has since transitioned through industrial, technological, scientific, and information revolutions. The world is now a very complex place where specialization dominates all fields. The executive branch now employs more than four million staff members, more people than there were in the entire United States at its inception. It is imperative that the qualifications for the presidency reflect the changing times and developments.

The job of the president is without question the most complex in the world. It should be observed that lawyers, doctors, engineers, teachers, nurses, and all professionals must go through rigorous years of training and complete an internship and a state board examination before they can qualify to serve in those fields. None of these professionals bear a burden comparable in scope and magnitude to that of the presidency. There used to be that saying that "Anybody can be president of the United States of America." That phrase needs to be retired immediately.

In addition to the stated qualifications in the Constitution, a president needs to demonstrate clear and convincing evidence that they can manage at the national and international levels. The president's reading/comprehension skills must be of a very high standard. Furthermore, they must demonstrate super high levels of listening skills. They must be able to process and assimilate information at unprecedented levels. There must also be clear and convincing evidence that the president is willing to be a lifelong learner. The president must be flexible and demonstrate the ability to earn the trust of all Americans, regardless of their many differences. Presidents must be ethically sound and be guided by a strong moral compass.

Additionally, as cited in Edwards, Wattenberg, and Lineberry (2016), Neuman points out that democratic theory has never been explicit about the precise requirements of knowledge and cognitive skills that must be exhibited by each citizen for the democratic system to work as intended. In light of the current wave of political apathy and the astonishing decline of political awareness, Congress must, at this time, establish what the electorate needs to know, understand, and be able to do to fulfill its democratic obligations. The nation's leading academic institutions should be entrusted with the task of determining the content of what the electorate needs to know, understand, and be able to do politically. The electorate must be given an opportunity to review and make inputs to this curriculum. After it is approved, Congress must then inspire a political revivalist movement to keep the United States in the vanguard of the democratic process.

Political ignorance should be addressed at all levels of the educational process. National requirements need to be set, and incentives offered to those who demonstrate depth and breadth of knowledge in the political process. Mandatory political studies as a pathway to most disciplines should be encouraged to help to instill patriotism and an understanding of the American political process. This would also inspire current and future young leaders to enter the political arena, as they could be taught that they can make a difference.

Furthermore, Congress should promote corporate buy-ins to these programs. Scholarships and other incentives to individuals who aspire to lead would make a significant difference in removing young people's political apathy. Corporate ethical and professional standards spread across the entire political spectrum would help to remove some of the current inappropriate behaviors exhibited by untrained political leaders.

The tyranny of political ignorance now threatening American liberty should be the stimulus that motivates the entire United States Congress to examine the state engine with its 330 million cylinders. Currently, the state engine runs with more than half its cylinders inhibited through ill health, lack of educational opportunities, systemic racism, discrimination, and a host of other impurities, including political apathy and political ignorance. The nation's engine was originally designed to run with inhibited cylinders. Now is Congress's opportunity to fix that anomaly. An awakened and enlightened Congress must come to realize that the Constitution made it the originator of the laws that govern the mechanics of the nation's political, economic, and social engine.

Regardless of how one assesses the United States' achievements since its birth to the present time, what is certain is that this nation is yet to achieve its full potential. That will be possible only when the state engine's cylinders are made to fire without inhibition. The synchronization of all these cylinders is Congress's challenge. Time is of the essence. Congresspersons should realize that this tune-up must be at the top of the policy agenda. It is a challenging task, but Congress can do it if it removes all the barriers and lets the engineers of all stripes conduct the orchestration. This would also be another step in removing systemic racism, which is currently all pervasive in the distribution of the nation's scarce resources.

Congress, in an effort to involve all 330 million inhabitants in the political, economic, and social development of the nation, needs to involve research that covers all segments of the population. Surveys should be conducted that determine what all groups are demanding of the government. This involves a monumental undertaking. The one-size-fits-all approach must be retired. After scientifically identifying all the various groups' needs, policymakers should engage technological gurus to feed this information into their supercomputers to determine what policies can and will work. All manner of possibilities may emerge. The policy entrepreneur concepts predicted by computers instead of bureaucrats would present multiple possibilities from which congressional policymakers could choose.

Through a system of elimination and trial and error, Congress could come up with computerized models that equitably involve all groups. When models are chosen, information should be made public, and individuals and groups should be educated to follow their progress over time and make recommendations. The brightest and the best minds would have opportunities to give input, and over time, the chosen templates would be modified to meet all the people's goals. Instant gratification must be tempered when these models are adapted. The transparency and accountability dilemmas would be solved once and for all when the ideal models emerge.

Computers are driving all processes today. It is time to involve computers in the policymaking process. It is time that Congress has access to information on every individual in the United States as it begins to shape policies to take the nation in a new direction. The coronavirus pandemic has removed the façade from the "greatest economy," and what is exposed is not a beautiful sight. The new policies must involve all Americans, and the inequities must be addressed and remedied once and for all.

The United States Congress has repelled threats to the nation before by using diplomacy backed by its economic and military might. However, the current threat to the United States' democracy challenges the very core of its people's values. Congress is equipped with oversight and override powers to help it to effectuate any new change that this threat may engender. As a first step, the United States Congress must push back on the president's political ignorance and bring the Constitution's checks and balances into play.

Lack of respect for the office of the presidency may be the most severe crack in the United States' democratic armor right now. There used to be a time when the office commanded a great deal of respect. Both political parties respected the office, regardless of the president's political party. The international community also had a high regard for the office because of the statue and bearing of the men who held it. Contenders valued the office and respected all aspirants to this noble position. Currently, the office is tarnished and severely damaged. It is going to require a great deal of hard work to restore it to its original status of strength and power. If this democracy survives Donald J. Trump, succeeding presidents will have some heavy lifting to do to restore national and international trust in the United States' leadership.

5

THE GREATEST
ECONOMY ON EARTH

It used to be that great minds allowed others to observe their greatness and heap encomiums on them. Great minds never praised themselves, for that was not the appropriate thing to do. Self-praise, they thought, was no recommendation. It was also thought that those who used this strategy had some inferiority complex and boasted to deflect and hide behind their shortcomings. The current United States president, Donald J. Trump, is probably the greatest threat ever to confront the United States' democracy. His natural proclivity to make himself the center of gravity as the nation's leader has limited his ability to elevate the interest and security of the United States above his personal interests. This trait also inhibits his ability to seriously follow the advice of exerts in his administration. It totally inhibits his ability to lead.

President Donald J. Trump never allows a moment to go by when he is not praising the United States' economy, under his administration, as the greatest economy in the world and the greatest of all time. Of course, he claims this economy as his own, even though objective observers know that economies are never built in three-year spans, the amount of time he has been in office. Probably, the inferiority complex here is the realization that it is really not his economy but that of his predecessor, Barack Obama.

President Barack Obama inherited an economy tethering on the brink of collapse when he assumed the presidency in 2009. He and his administration pulled the economy back from the edge of the precipice, using strategies that were condemned by most members of the then-opposition Republican Party. Thereafter, the economy inched its way back with each succeeding year. The growth was slow but steady, and the unemployment percentage of the population decreased year by year. When Donald Trump assumed the presidency, the economy was steadily improving. President Trump hopped on to an economic train already gaining momentum. It is a fact that the economic train gained traction and velocity, but President Trump cannot prove that this would not have happened regardless of who succeeded Barack Obama. Another way to challenge President Trump's economic acumen is to examine his lack of an alternative proposal in the face of the coronavirus pandemic. Where is President Trump's plan B if plan A falters? It has been more than nine months now since the coronavirus pandemic crippled the United States' economy, but there is no plan except going back to the failed approach that exposes a huge portion of the population to health hazards, hunger, homelessness, and police abuse and assault on a daily basis. Where is the economic plan to address all the people's needs?

An objective analysis of the greatest economy today and the greatest the world has ever seen would pose some serious questions. For example, by what criteria do you arrive at this conclusion? If one criterion is the health of the inhabitants, then the greatest economy on earth would come up woefully short. An estimated twenty million Americans have no health insurance at all. They fear going to the doctor or to the emergency room, for they cannot afford the cost of their health care. They suffer in silence and are likely to die from diseases that normally do not kill when proper medical attention is available. Those who do have insurance perpetually worry about the insurance company's power to deny claims at the most critical junctures in their health care maintenance.

The coronavirus pandemic has exposed the shortcomings of the United States' social, political, and economic experiment. Cries for help can be heard from all segments of the United States' population. This national disaster is radically different from previous experiences. This is probably explained by the fact that previous disasters were localized and did not affect all parts of the country simultaneously and with the same devastating intensity. Within a month of its manifestation on United States soil, however, the coronavirus pandemic signaled that no corner of the country would be spared its wrath. Because other countries were devastated by the coronavirus before it actually hit the United States, it makes the collective response of this country remarkably ineffective. It is also shocking that the United States is not a leader in this recovery but is trailing the rest of the developed economies. President Trump was elected in 2016 to prevent this eventuality, but his political ignorance is beginning to affect all facets of American life.

In fact, the initial response to the coronavirus pandemic at the national level was horrible. The United States president was in the throes of an embarrassing impeachment trial, and his anger was scorching. He was never one for clear and analytical thinking in the first place, and the impeachment saga had him in a mood programmed for vengeance. Those civil servants who cataloged and reported the President's out-of-line behavior would pay dearly. With his fury at the Democratic Party at fever pitch, President Trump immediately characterized the impending coronavirus disease as a Democratic hoax and articulated this on national television at one of his frenetic political rallies. President Trump did this even though he had privileged information that the coronavirus was air borne and far more deadly that the flu.

For President Trump, the coronavirus disease could not have arrived at a more inconvenient time. With his reelection foremost on his mind and fresh from his exoneration in the impeachment saga, he was ready to sing praises to his great economic success. He was not about to allow this disease to steal his show. He downplayed the disease and assured the nation, without any proof, that the disease would quickly disappear. He literally wished the disease away. The fifteen identified cases would be reduced to zero, and the heat would take care of the coronavirus disease over the summer; those were his predictions. These responses coming from a United States president regarding an approaching disaster are very frightening. The fallacious prediction of fifteen cases has materialized to more than eight million real coronavirus infections, and over 220, 000 Americans are dead as a result of President Trump's casual assessment of the coronavirus pandemic.

One is left to wonder if the threat of an impending nuclear threat would have been treated any differently. There is sufficient evidence to conclude that if the nuclear threat emanated from Russia, President Trump would hesitate to take control and defend the nation. President Trump has never admitted any negatives about his supposed friend Vladimir Putin. If past behavior predicts future behavior, the United States is precariously poised in terms of national security.

The national response to the coronavirus pandemic was predicated on President Donald J. Trump's ineptitude and his astonishing disregard for scientific solutions. In the president's bungling in the face of a national crisis, multiple cracks in the United States' democratic armor became evident. It became palpably clear that President Trump was not aware of the critical elements of the preamble of the United States Constitution, particularly the element that stresses the promotion of the general welfare. The coronavirus pandemic gave President Trump an opportunity to grab the reins of the country, invoke all the powers invested in him by the Constitution, contain the coronavirus pandemic, and demonstrate to the world that the United States is still a world class leader. President Trump failed on this account.

Instead of leading the fifty states, President Trump blamed them for not having stockpiles of materials to fight the disease. The framers of the Constitution met in Philadelphia in 1787 to address the issue of the thirteen states' inability to manage crises at the national level. The whole purpose of the Constitutional Convention was to design a political arrangement that would address the states' shortcomings. The office of the presidency was created to direct operations in the event of a national crisis. The nation has never faced a crisis more fearsome than the coronavirus pandemic. Nor has it ever experienced the level of presidential dereliction of duty demonstrated by President Trump. The coronavirus disease is an invisible enemy, and its killing potential is inestimable. Instead of taking control and addressing the coronavirus pandemic as a national priority, President Donald J. Trump managed to take the United States back in time to pre 1787. The tyranny of political ignorance peaked at that moment, and the coronavirus pandemic rages on.

President Trump's management during the coronavirus pandemic deferred most actions to the states. This signified a total lack of understanding of the Constitution and the responsibilities entrusted to his office as president. President Trump had to be reminded that he had the power to call up the Army Corps of Engineers and the National Guard to help to fight the coronavirus disease. He hesitated to invoke the Defense Production Act, and when he did, it was for a brief period—too brief. The Defense Production Act should have remained active until the coronavirus disease abated. The president's overall performance in this national crisis has been pathetic, to say the least.

President Trump has become fixated with the positive performance of the economy since he assumed office. He is a president who is more concerned with his reelection than the people's welfare. He seems not to be able to focus on more than one issue at time, despite his frequent boast that he does everything better than everyone else. In fact, on numerous occasions, he claimed that he and only he can solve the nation's problems. His limitations are now exposed by the coronavirus pandemic.

The coronavirus pandemic blew the façade off the United States' political, social, and economic achievements. President Trump has one goal, and that is for the economy to return to normal even though the coronavirus pandemic is signaling to him and to the United States people that "normal" has failed and is now untenable. The solutions will have to be radically different and revolutionary. The solutions are not in President Trump's toolbox.

President Trump, as the nation's leader, was expected to put the people and not himself first. He was expected to use the coronavirus pandemic to showcase the United States' world leadership acumen. President Trump failed to perceive the coronavirus pandemic as a warning that the nation has not been on the right course in terms of political, economic, and social equality. However, he was too absorbed with his self-image to notice. A leader with vision would have taken precautions as set out in the pandemic playbook left by his predecessor. President Trump probably brushed the playbook aside as he did all of his predecessor's achievements.

When the coronavirus went after the poor blacks, Hispanics, Native American and other minorities, a real leader would have formed a series of task forces with express commands. One task force would study the economic situation of these people and make recommendations to fix the glaring inequities once and for all. Another task force would look at the health care disparity between the white, black, and minority workers and make recommendations. Yet another would look at the possibility of giving all Americans a health care coverage that matches the one President Trump and all congresspersons have. Another would be focused on how to protect the population while the CDC and other scientists go in search of a cure or vaccine to knock out the coronavirus disease. There should have been a deluge of task forces. The American people would know that the president could not possibly accomplish all of these goals, but they would see his effort, and they would know that he cares. If he achieved just one or two of these goals, he would go down in history as one of the great presidents. Instead, President Trump's response to the coronavirus pandemic places him at the bottom of the pile of United States presidents in descending order of worth.

What America needed in the crisis engendered by the coronavirus pandemic was a leader who would hear them and listen to their cry. However, President Trump did no such thing. He placed all the emphasis on himself and on this great economy that he did not build, even though he thought he did. Objective thinkers know who built that economy. With Americans dying around him like flies every day,

President Trump kept calling for the reopening of the economy. This made him out to be a president without empathy. It is hard for President Trump to project what he does not have inside of himself or does not understand, but he could have tried. In all this suffering, he has not once shown empathy or displayed any form of humility. President Trump was a reality television star; he could have put on a show. He might have gotten away with it.

America in crisis needs a leader who can mobilize and harness all the capabilities that lie dormant in the nation. President Trump had to be prodded to call out the Army Corps of Engineers in the coronavirus crisis, and they were not used to their maximum potential because the president's focus was not on the dying Americans but on his economy. The president has yet to call on academia for solutions because he is under the false assumption that he and only he can solve the nation's problems. The people elected Donald J. Trump because he was supposed to be this successful real estate tycoon, a very successful businessman. He is yet to bring this acumen to the presidency, except perhaps in the self-aggrandizement arena. As a builder of great edifices, the electorate expected him to build and not to wreck. His wrecking skills are taking preeminence over his building and uniting capabilities.

When the coronavirus pandemic blew away the façade and exposed the nation's real economic character, all Americans realized that new solutions were called for. Going back to normal was not an option. They were horrified when the president kept insisting on opening up the economy and get it going again. A forward-looking leader would explore innovative solutions to the problem. During the Democratic primary, Andrew Yang had a proposal to bolster family income by giving the head of household in every family $1,000 per month. It looked far-fetched at the time, but when the coronavirus pandemic blew away the façade and exposed the greatest economy, it suddenly looked like a possible solution. Andrew Yang's proposal would require the president and his billionaire friends to sacrifice a little. Would that be asking too much? Calling up Andrew Yang as an adviser would have made President Trump look like a problem solver.

Bernie Sanders had enlightened proposals to match the changing dynamics of the times and the population. The coronavirus pandemic's removal of the greatest economic façade makes Bernie Sanders relevant. Education and health care are rights that all Americans must have. It would help to study Bernie Sanders's student loan proposals. American students and graduates are crippled by the burden of student loans. Release them from their burden, Mr. President, and they will be able to propel your economy to heights unknown. Study Bernie Sanders's proposal to give Medicare to all Americans and eventually get rid of the insurance companies that have abused their privileged monopolies for centuries. The inequities that the coronavirus pandemic exposed must be addressed. Ignoring all of these glaring needs implies that the people must solve their own problems. They will do just that by voting in an administration with a mandate to address these age long anomalies.

President Trump's disdain for science makes him look backward and weak. The nonsense that he uttered about injecting disinfectants in citizens' bodies to knock out the coronavirus disease puts him squarely in the realm of fools. The president of the United States should not say that even if it crosses his mind. Many of his utterances and actions make him look ridiculous. For example, his own task force determined that masks are useful in protecting against the coronavirus pandemic. His Vice President heads the task force, yet the president has refused to wear a mask. He does not realize how monumentally stupid that makes him look. Even worse, he forbade others around him to wear masks as well, and that sends the message to his followers that they can flaunt the mask-wearing rule. The president in this respect is an enabler of the coronavirus pandemic.

President Trump's inordinately slow response to the coronavirus and his politicization of the masks make him guilty of aiding and abetting the spread of the deadly coronavirus disease. Mr. President, wise men think alike. President Trump, by not wearing a mask, sends a lot of messages to the American people. It may be okay to be a fool who exposes himself to this deadly disease, but it is not okay to transmit your disease to innocent Americans who happen to be in your presence.

Mr. President, you have contracted the virus because you want to, but transmitting it to others is stupid and cruel. You had already proved that you were not capable of empathy. You are forgiven for that. It is an upbringing shortcoming. Refusing to wear the mask and encouraging huge segments of the population to follow your lead is simply inhumane. Holding political rallies where social distancing and mask wearing are not mandatory is plain insanity.

6

SYSTEMIC RACISM

M r. President, you and a lot of the people you surround yourself with, including William Barr, the Attorney General, do not believe that systemic racism is an all-pervasive variable in American life. Some others who support your thinking and your actions do not believe there is systemic racism either. For that, the people who are objective thinkers can forgive you all. You see, Mr. President, there are parallel school systems in the United States of America. There are also parallel curricula. It is possible that you never had a single black or minority student in class with you throughout your education. It is very likely that your curriculum did not place priority on black and minority history. You most likely did not have to ask why because you heard your parents, neighbors, and acquaintances telling you why, and you probably did not have the savvy to find out on your own. The following paragraphs may serve to enlighten you and your likeminded aides and supporters.

Mr. President, systemic racism exists where all the people, by design, do not have the same opportunities. Skin color and poverty blocked many students from attending the schools you attended. On your election campaign, you addressed an African American gentleman as "My African American." You may be forgiven for that, but systemic racism made the black person property because white supremacist plantation owners disqualified him as a human being. "My African American" is reminiscent of those times, Mr. President. It is reported that you once said that you would never "allow a black person to count your money." Ignorance could be blamed for such remarks too, but it is part of the systemic racism process—belittle and dominate. Mr. President, you used the phrase "dominate the streets and control those thugs" on several occasions. You sounded very much like the white supremacist plantation owners who stripped black people of every shred of dignity and humanity. *Dominate and control them* is a four-hundred-year-old refrain familiar to black people. The white supremacist planters used this methodology for fear of rebellion by black slaves. Your call to dominate the streets of Washington sounded like your slaves were in rebellion.

Your behavior and that of your aides and supporters suggests that you have very little knowledge about the House of Burgesses in Virginia between 1619 and 1670. If you did, you would know that within a year of the arrival of the first Africans in Jamestown, Virginia (1619), a group of white British settlers, all Christian men, met in the church building in that town (1620) to discuss the fate of future African arrivals. Over the one-year period, these white Christian men came to the conclusion that the Africans were a subhuman species that could not possibly live freely among the superior white race. They decided there and then that all future African arrivals must enter as slaves, owned by white individuals in the Virginia colony.

In subsequent years between 1620 and 1670, the House of Burgesses passed several other laws stripping the black slaves of all rights and their humanity. President Trump, the other slave-owning colonies, in subsequent years, adopted the Virginia slave-owning template. Yes, President Trump, the white man's knee has been on the black man's neck for four hundred years. Your aides say you do not read much, and your attention span is short; therefore, this brief bit of history should suffice. It is hoped that you are capable of learning something new in your late years. Your aides and your supporters may learn something from this too.

For the aides and the supporters of President Trump, it is hoped that you have longer attention spans. The slave patrol that hounded down the runaway slaves had an obligation to return the slave to his master alive because he was valuable property. The present law enforcement establishment in the United States has its genesis in the slave patrol. The difference is that current law enforcement officers do not have to bring the black man in alive. With the emancipation of the slaves, that came to an abrupt end. The arresting officer is often judge, jury, and executioner. George Floyd was accused of possessing and passing a counterfeit twenty-dollar bill. He was tried and executed on the spot in public view in broad daylight. President Trump is proud to be head of that establishment. The law-and-order president. Do some more thinking on what you sound so proud to be, Mr. President.

Mr. President, you often proclaim that you are the law-and-order president. These are not words to boost your ego. They are to demonstrate knowledge of the Constitution of the United States. Moreover, a law-and-order president makes sure that these words are enforceable. The Fifth Amendment states, "Nor shall any person be deprived of life, limb or property, without due process of law." Mr. President, that means that the police officers are duty bound to bring the accused person to court. A thousand killings by police annually indicates that there is no law and order. That is chaos, plain and simple. A law-and-order president would spend a portion of each day encouraging the citizenry to be temperate and law enforcement officials to be cognizant of the law.

During your 2016 election campaign, you gave the impression that you would be the very opposite of law and order. You encouraged the police officers not to be too gentle with detainees. Aren't suspects supposed to be innocent until proven guilty in a court of law, Mr. President? A law-and-order president who sees only a few bad apples in a police establishment that kills more than one thousand Americans annually must himself be one of those bad apples. When you saw good people on both sides of the murderous protests in Charlottesville in Virginia, you were not a good apple. You were not a good apple when you encouraged your supporters to punch protestors, with a promise to pay their court costs. When you said the golfers who shouted, "White power!" to people protesting your incompetence were "great people," you were a bad apple.

You watched George Floyd's murder on television, all eight minutes and forty-six seconds of it. That is one that was caught on camera. How many were not on camera, Mr. Law-and-Order President? You, as the law-and-order president, should disavow that killing and rebuke the force under your command in no uncertain manner. Instead, at one of your news conferences, you promised never to do anything to weaken police power. The people and education will.

The people on the streets are calling for justice in George Floyd's murder. In situations like these, you boasted that you are the only one who can fix it. So far, America has not seen you do anything about the people's call for justice. You issued an executive order, but it did not contain one element of what the people on the streets are seeking. You already got a lesson in systemic racism. You did not address that issue. You could not because you do not believe it exists. This means that you really cannot deal with this issue. It is okay to say you can't manage this problem because it is too personal for you. If you recuse yourself, the people will move on and find their own solutions. One thing is certain: the people will get what they want. Justice! If it does not come immediately, it does not matter; they will never rest until they get it. They might have to vote you out of office to get it done. That they will do in the 2020 election.

7

THE CATACLYSMIC COLLISION

The coronavirus pandemic was in the process of exposing the many cracks in the United States' democratic armor when a Minneapolis police officer killed George Floyd by kneeling on his neck for eight minutes and forty-eight seconds in broad daylight. George Floyd's death also reveals cracks in the nation's democratic armor. The entire gruesome drama was beamed on national television. Both cataclysmic occurrences will impact broad swaths of the United States population for generations to come. These occurrences will highlight some of the great accomplishments of the United States people as they struggle to achieve the equality goals embedded in the Declaration of Independence and in the Fourteenth Amendment of the Constitution.

Additionally, they will also bring many of the nation's failures into sharper focus. Both events represent another chance for the United States government to put partisan politics aside and address the nation's political, economic, and social failures. The equality goals of the Declaration of Independence and the Fourteenth Amendment of the Constitution cannot be achieved without bold legislative initiatives by the United States Congress.

When the white police officer kneed George Floyd to death on the street in Minneapolis in broad daylight, it was videotaped and beamed across the world. The killing lifted the veil of hypocrisy that shrouded the practice of systemic racism and social inequality. The Black Lives

Matter movement sprang into action and mobilized the entire nation in protests. The streets of the nation filled up with marchers in every major city in the United States to protest the killing. Teachers and college and university professors sat up and took notice. Some joined the marchers.

Surviving civil rights activists blinked to clear their eyes. The nationwide marches looked familiar to them, but the demographic mix of marchers was different this time around. The demographic mix was reminiscent of the late Doctor Martin Luther King's prophesy in the "I Have a Dream Speech," in which he envisioned the children of all the races mingling in harmony. On the streets of the United States, the "out of many one people" motto was realized. The challenge now is to move it throughout the society. The marchers pledged to stay on the street until justice is served and the inequities are addressed.

The demographic mix supporting the civil rights
movement was quite impressive.

All big businesses took notice too and began to realize that operations would not be the same anymore. Lawmakers quaked in their boots, for they realized that the marchers' light was focused on them. They knew that they had to act or be pushed into obscurity. President Trump knew not what to do. His lack of historical knowledge made him see the crowds and the Black Lives Matter movement as symbols of hate. He took refuge in his bunker.

There were others too, including little children and some older folks. The mothers of victims of police brutality groaned and died another death. Athletes, artists, singers, and musicians felt proud that they had used their privileged platforms to focus the light on the nation's racism and social inequalities. The seeds they sowed were germinating and growing lustily.

Finally, the electorate at home, at work, and on the streets looked for action and began their assessments. Their decisions will be greatly influenced by the marchers on the streets and the response of the elected leaders. Both occurrences give the nation a moment to pause and reflect on what has been done well and what needs to be done right now to bring the nation closer to the equality paradigm, posed as a challenge at the nation's inception in the Declaration of Independence. The electorate is also focused on the "equal protection under law" clause of the Fourteenth Amendment.

The following paragraphs will look at some critical players in the nation's development and offer them words of congratulations and encouragement. The paragraphs will also recommend what these players must continue to do to push back against the tyranny of political ignorance that enveloped the nation with the election of President Donald Trump and to mend the cracks in the United States' democratic armor. Progress in the march to equality is incremental; it is guided by gradualism. The pressure on elected officials must be relentless in order to bring Americans of all races and gender closer to the equality goals of the Declaration of Independence and the equal protection clause of the Fourteenth Amendment.

The Nation's Mothers

Good mothers, you are mothers of all. You do not feel the pain of loss in color. You just feel it. For good mothers, grief is an inherent quality. Good black mothers in the United States have never not grieved. They were separated from their children at the moment of captivity in Africa. As slaves on American soil, their children were sold without a moment's notice when their owners needed cash. Black mothers live every day expecting grief, for that is what they have known from time immemorial. Their mental stability is a tribute to their unflappable determination to give their children a better future than the life they themselves experienced.

Grief comes through death by natural causes, accidents, inner-city violence, drive-by shootings, senseless squabbles, and worst of all by the police hired to protect society. The police killers are usually white, and the victims are usually black. Police killing is not new. The methods of killing vary from lynching, to shooting, to chokehold and kneeling on the neck. Direct grief tears at the heart. Vicarious grief makes all black mothers the mothers of all the victims of police killings. Vicarious grief tears at the soul.

Black mothers' emotional fortitude is unfathomable and incomprehensible. They are forced to create double personalities. They have to pretend that life goes on. They also have to practice fortifying against bad news, for every time another mother loses a child, they die too. Good mothers die a thousand deaths. They go to work and carry out their duties, but they never get over the emotional devastation that comes with the loss of a child at the hand of law enforcement officers. Posttraumatic stress disorder is a permanent feature of their lives, an ever-present companion. Good mothers create outlets to take care of their pain. Some find it in their religion; others lean on family and friends. A special class of good mothers look for meaning within themselves and elsewhere. They believe they can make a differences. They become activists for the cause of all grieving mothers. They bury their dead and set about preventing other deaths.

Some good mothers head some of the movements that are teaching other mothers how to prepare their children to react in police encounters and walk away alive. Others form groups to teach grieving mothers how to cope. These groups petition the government at the local, state, and national levels to address the issue of police killing black and other minority children in their homes and on the streets of America. Other groups educate mothers of victims of police killings and guide them to support groups.

The double calamity of the coronavirus pandemic and the white police officer kneeling on George Floyd's neck for eight minutes and forty seconds while he begged for air and died crying for his mother shook you like nothing ever did. All good mothers, dead and alive, heard George Floyd's last call for "Mama." Just when you thought you had seen it all, the coronavirus came singling out black people because four centuries of systemic racism made them prime targets for the ravages of this invisible scourge. Now, black mothers, you must teach your children how to survive two scourges.

You are not without hope though, for the years you have been praying and participating in teaching others to cope and coming together to support one another are beginning to bear fruits. The streets of the United States are filled with hope. Your kids seem to have been listening to your teachings

The demographic mix in the Black Lives Matter marches was much greater than that of the civil rights marches.

They must have been doing more than listening, for their friends of all colors and ethnicities are in the streets with them. The demographics on the streets in support of Black Lives Matter tells you that the times are a changing. The generations of the future will not be tolerating white supremacists' abuse forever. Your kids recognize a crack in the United States' democratic armor, and they are pledging to become crack menders even under the tyranny of political ignorance. They are going to be the change they are asking for. The change will not come overnight, but it is coming, and all the good mothers can continue praying, supporting, educating, and preparing their children for a new tomorrow. You can say with assurance, "Thank God almighty, my children and grandchildren will see a brighter day." Their children will not fall through the cracks so long as they continue to protest and to understand that change will not come all at once. They will learn the incremental character of change and the truth that it must be relentlessly pursued.

The Nation's Educators, Past and Present

Greetings to all educators! You try to teach the words of Thomas Jefferson as written in the Declaration of Independence: "We hold these truths to be self-evident, that all men (people) are created equal, that they are endowed by their Creator with certain unalienable rights; that among these are life, liberty, and the pursuit of happiness." Your first challenge was to convince black and minority students that they belong and are part of the equality paradigm. These groups had difficulty finding themselves in the "We the People" opening phrase of the Constitution's preamble. The society around them did not reflect their belonging. Some of your female students also struggled to find themselves in the equality pronouncements, as they were excluded from most fields of endeavor in a male-dominated society. As great educators, you plodded on though, knowing that time is a critical variable in the transmission of ideas. The passage of the Nineteenth Amendment and the civil rights movement helped you to convince these groups that the equality time clock is working on their behalf. You have overcome many hurdles as you educate the nation's young people.

Currently, the classes you teach are usually filled with young people who seem distracted by their technological gadgets. They do not complete your assignments at the high expectation levels you set for them. Some do not do the assignments at all. You try to explain to them that Thomas Jefferson knew that the states he was creating with these words did not immediately meet the equality goals of the Declaration of Independence. Rather, he was giving the new nation goals to strive for in the years to come. As brilliant professionals, you do your research and investigate best practices to get your students to show even a modicum of interest. You collaborate with other teachers, but the constant refrain is political apathy. Your students are not interested in your lessons because the nature of partisan politics does not give them the impression that they can make a difference. The good thing it that you are not the type to ever give up.

Moreover, great educators do not teach for the moment. They do not teach and look for instant gratification. Dave Brubaker reminds educators that when they shine external lights on students, they sometimes do not learn because they are not ready. Educators must never be dissuaded by this. They must continue to teach, knowing that one day the students' inner light will be turned on. That is when the teachers' words and strategies come into play. Great educators teach for tomorrow when the students' light sparks. That is when students need that fallback-on variable, all the lessons educators taught and thought fell on deaf ears. If educators stop teaching, students would be lost when that inner light comes on and they are groping for meaning. Great educators know that their students hear them years later and not necessarily at the time they speak.

To the political science educators and especially government teachers, the lessons you taught on the structure and functions of government did not fall on deaf ears. Your students know when to rise to the occasion and put their knowledge of the Constitution on display. They are fully aware of their First Amendment rights, and they role-played it for the nation on national television in the Black Lives Matter protests. Rest assured that your encouragement to students to seek careers that can help make a difference will be respected. Some of those who did not show promise in particular disciplines will probably find their niche in being activists who will plug away at do-nothing legislators and make them uncomfortable until they are forced to perform or be voted into oblivion.

As you watched your students on the streets of the United States, demanding equality, justice, and an opportunity to be heard, you must have been electrified. You probably recognized some of them. Yes, the death of George Floyd brought all the lessons you taught flooding back in your students' heads. For, it is true; a picture speaks a thousand words. What you taught for years on end was clarified in eight minutes and forty-six seconds as your present and former students watched a human life being snuffed out in the street. Your students were paying a lot more attention than you give them credit for. Educators now realize that their students can multitask very well; they are great at being inattentive and learning at the same time.

They not only march on the streets of the United States of America, demanding an end to systemic racism, bigotry, and injustice, but they are making recommendations to the nation's lawmakers and promising to become the change if nothing is done to redress the inexorable tide of police murder of black people. You are pumped up and ready to continue the great task of educating the nation's kids and reminding them that the United States fought against tyranny before and won. This time, the victory over the tyranny of political ignorance will come not with guns but with education and the vote. Good luck in all your endeavors. You have been great crack menders, and the nation needs you to continue the arduous process of teaching in a heterogeneous society.

The Civil Rights Activists, Past and Present

All of you took shelter in the "stay at home" command of the Centers for Disease Control (CDC), perplexed at what is taking place in the greatest economy in the world. You watched Blacks, Hispanics, Native Americans, and other minorities dying in disproportionate relations to other groups. It was another slap in the face for these groups, as systemic racism heightened the social and economic inequities in the American society. Your despondency levels are very high. Despite all this, it is easy to imagine some of your actions and feelings when you watched the national response to George Floyd's murder on national television.

For some of you, your minds wanted to get out there and join the marchers in the Black Lives Matter protests, but your bodies held you back because the energy component is not there anymore. Your elation, though, was uncontainable. Some of you were around with Dr. Martin Luther King and helped him to mobilize the people and harness resources to get issues addressed at the local, state, and national levels of government. Others of you faced assaults and beating in your struggles for human rights, justice, and equality. John Lewis was among those beaten to a pulp because he dared to fight for the right of black people's vote. The Black Lives Matter marches gave John Lewis one last moment to be on the streets, for in that movement, he was assured that the *conscience of Congress* would be immortalized. Shalom to those who have passed on before this glorious moment in American history!

You have watched two generations of Americans receive an education under desegregation. Children of all colors and ethnicity and religious beliefs have been educated in the United States' desegregated public school system. Black kids, white kids, and kids of every race and ethnicity interacted in public schools and debunked the myth that segregation was the only viable method of educating American students. Additionally, affirmative action and other equalizers that you fought for have opened up some whites-only institutions and given minorities access. Blacks and other minorities have graduated from these institutions, qualified to perform in all fields of endeavor.

Some have taken their places as lawyers, physicians, engineers, managers, judges in the legal system, in politics at the local, state, and national levels, and in a host of other fields. The changes have also produced one black president of the United States in the person of Barack Obama. All of these individuals are making their contributions and helping to remove some of the past stigma falsely pinned on blacks and minorities. Little by little, the barriers are coming down, and Americans are observing that all individuals of all races and ethnicities are capable of performing at the highest levels, if given the opportunities.

There may have been moments when you thought that the civil rights movement and its achievements were petering out. That is okay too, because you may sometime forget, like the Rev. Dr. Martin Luther King did in his "I Have a Dream" speech, that gradualism is an indispensable variable in the search for justice. The timeless characteristics of the state and its apparent slow but extraordinary ability to accommodate change have gradually prepared oppressed Americans to claim the equality goals set forth in the Declaration of Independence. What has been happening in these two generations of desegregated schooling is that the old white supremacist guards are dying off. Technology and education are illuminating their hiding places and their nefarious practices and flushing them out.

Yet there is much work to be done, for the genes of white supremacists permeate law enforcement establishments, which are protected by a supposed law-and-order President who understands nothing whatsoever about the search for equality and justice. Victory is in sight, but the battle is not over. It is critical to understand this stage of the battle because it is here that complacency is likely to set in. There is no room for complacency. The banner must be raised high until justice and equality become the victor's crown.

Yours and Dr. King's work set the stage for the generations of educated blacks and minority Americans. One has already assumed the presidency of the United States and has become an example that will be emulated in the years ahead. The stage is being set for a black female to become the next Vice President of the United States. This position is one step away from the presidency. Currently, women leaders are creating waves around the world with their forthrightness, their quiet dignity, and their superior negotiating acumen. It may be a woman who will put the finishing touches on the equality paradigm and usher in a season of justice to temper the current episode of tyranny engendered by political ignorance. Kamala Harris is steeped in jurisprudence and has been fighting for the causes of the oppressed. Her new platform could signal great strides on the road to real equality and justice under law for the downtrodden classes.

Take pride in the fact that you are the initiators of the movements that have brought the oppressed and neglected thus far. Do not underestimate your role in the present protests and the demands for justice and reform in this nation. Be thankful for your longevity and be strong in the knowledge that you have mended a few constitutional cracks on your journey. Stand firm and continue to inspire younger generations of activists who will take the baton to the next post in the race to end the tyranny of political ignorance.

Singers and Musicians

Peace and love to all singers and musicians. Shakespeare wrote, "If music be the food of love, play on." People in all of history have sung. Music is in the wind, in the stream, in the birds' call, in the animals' call, and in the insects' too. People have also invented music and all types of musical instruments. Music soothes the soul. Some singers and musicians immortalized themselves by leaving their creations for all generations. They are the comforters of the ages.

The black slaves brought nothing with them except their songs and their music when they were unceremoniously dragged to American soil. Everything, including their person, was taken from them, but no one could take their songs and their music. In this strange land, all they had were their voices and their music. When the work was backbreaking, they sang a song. When they grieved, and they did that a lot, they sang a song too. They had songs of love and songs of grief. They sang freedom songs a lot. They had redemption songs too. Music and songs were the balms of slavery.

Some churches were allowed to preach to the slaves. Some slaves had their own religion, but others attached themselves to Christian churches. This was a great experience for some slaves. Some religious denominations in the United States today have a strong black connection dating back to the slavery epoch. Blacks developed their own form of religious music, which became a vehicle for many of them to develop their own ministries. The black spiritual musical form and jazz, blues, and other genres became dominant forms of black music in the United States. Black music has influenced all forms of music all over the world. All these music and songs formats have been used to convey messages of hope in the struggle for equality and justice. Many famous black singers, dating back to the early years of the twentieth century, had their roots in gospel music. Many of them sang their way to fame and glory, but they never forgot to use their unique platforms to inspire change. One current black musician sang a tribute to the first responders in the coronavirus pandemic, bringing much relief in the dark days of this dreaded disease. Musicians are singing in this moment as they try to endure the tyranny of political ignorance. Listen to their songs, as the days of freedom are approaching. Follow the sound of their music out of this wilderness of death and destruction.

The United States Athletes, Past and Present

Greetings to all the United States' great athletes! The United States athletes have been bastions of support for the oppressed nationally and internationally. You have been exceptional in bringing joy, elation, and exuberance to local, national, and international populations. The nation observes how your talents have brought personal, familial, and national fame and glory. Future athletes draw from your discipline in arduous training and your ability to remain focused on the highest standards. What is most remarkable about you is that you use your privileged platforms for the good of the downtrodden and the underprivileged.

Some of you stood up and spoke when you were expected to be silent. Others of you defied government edicts to become advocates for oppressed humanity, nationally and internationally. You have used your elevated platform to shine light on injustices here in the United States and around the world. You have fought against racism and political, economic, and social injustices. Some of you have sacrificed your medals and your fortunes to make a point when racism has reared its ugly head. Others of you rejected the United States military draft to make your case for the cause of peace for humanity. The nation took note of those of you who kneeled for justice at the risk of losing your position on the team and a loss of income. You and your families faced abuse because of your stand, but that did not deter you one bit. You believed in yourself and your cause. You will see the tide turn, and you will be recognized for being ahead of your time.

You have become famous role models for using your privileged platform for the good of the downtrodden. Some of you have lived to see the changes you fought for materialize in your own lifetime. Others of you were recognized posthumously, but the effect is the same; the changes came about because of you. Your charitable contributions are helping to mend some of the cracks in the United States' democratic armor. Many underprivileged children have food, shelter, education, and security because of the work you do to help to redress some the inequities in the society. The coronavirus pandemic and the murder of George Floyd on the streets of Minneapolis suggest that you still have a lot of work to do to bring about equality and justice for all.

Businesses

Businesspeople may have a sense of pride or a sense of guilt as they watch the diversity of marchers in the Black Lives Matter protests on the streets of the United States. For the enlightened business owners, the myth that black people are a subhuman species was debunked in your places of business. Some of you hired people of all genders and races and helped to satisfy the equal opportunity employer component of the Civil Rights Act. Some of your minority workers have taken your businesses to heights unknown. It was their way of reciprocating, for you helped to remove unjustified stigmas. Others of you foster work environments where employees have opportunities to grow and develop their social and intellectual skills. The solidarity of the races displayed on the streets of the United States in protest of the police killing of George Floyd in broad daylight is, in part, the result of the training and workplace operating procedures. Continue your good work and move the equality march to the next level.

Many business firms are watching their clientele marching on the streets in search of justice and equality. The work is not over for those of you who practice appropriate workplace ethics and behavior. There is a great deal of work to be done. Sometimes blacks and minorities are seen only in the lower echelons of your establishments or not at all. If this fits your work environment, you need to find ways to make your administrative and management staff reflect the general population. You must understand that the protests in progress are but a beginning. Institutional racism must not be present in your establishment at any level. The marchers are serious about justice and equality, and they will eventually target businesses that are openly engaging in unfair and unequal practices. No business will survive the boycott of those protestors on the streets of America.

Some businesses are ignorant of their labels and what they portend for blacks and other minorities. It is time to do your research and be sensitive to the practices that may yield a profit at the expense of your employees and your patrons. Be sensitive about where you put your advertisement dollars and where your endorsements go. Others of you can become involved at all levels of the nation's educational developments. Offering a scholarship, no matter how small, can be a great help to needy students. Tracking students through college or identifying their talents and offering them positions in your businesses upon completion of their training is a positive way to give back to the community in which you do business.

Some of you may be large enough to adopt a school in your neighborhood and help to mend the cracks in the nation's democracy. Students develop many skills when they have opportunities for on-the-job training. Many of the very poor Blacks, Hispanics, and other minorities do not know what career choices to make because they do not have family role models. On-the-job training experiences can help them to find role models in your businesses. No matter how profitable your business is at the present time, a more educated workforce and clientele will only redound to the good of your businesses. Observe the marches on the streets of the United States and make sure that you are making community-conscious modifications and are moving to eradicate systemic racism and bigotry. You can continue to help and force the tyranny of political ignorance to its demise.

Lawmakers

Yours is an unenviable position. You have been blamed for inaction throughout the development of the United States' political, economic, and social experiment. It is not without reason. One thing is certain: it was the lawmaking body in Jamestown, Virginia, specifically the House of Burgesses, that created the white supremacist movement that initiated the beginnings of slavery and the oppression of black people in this land. It must be the lawmaking body, Congress that brings these nefarious practices to an end. You have it within your power to initiate that change. First you must put your country above partisan politics, invoke your congressional oversight and override powers, and lay down the laws that will eradicate the inequalities that have come to dominate the society. Some of you have yielded completely to a president's power, abdicating you responsibilities to the people of the United States and forgetting your status as coequal branches of the government.

Do not squander the gift of the dual cataclysmic occurrences before you right now. The coronavirus pandemic and the police murder of George Floyd have exposed your years of receiving salaries under false pretenses. The social inequalities that the coronavirus exposed are the result of years of neglect and failure to address the plight of the poor and the oppressed. George Floyd's death is the outcome of generations of unfettered systemic racism. You must immediately address these issues in meaningful ways. The people on the streets of America have spoken. You know their demands. Whatever you do, do not take the protesters for granted.

Some of you are deadly afraid of President Donald Trump and what he can do to your careers. He can only do that if you fail to use the collective power of the House in which you serve. At some stage, you have to put away your wimpy behavior and put on the armor of real men and real women and stand up to President Trump for the good of the nation. Some of you have forgotten to be independent thinkers with your own sense of value and worth. Donald Trump has imposed his obnoxious values on some of you, and you have yielded without a fight. Be true to yourselves and use the powers of the Constitution to regain your status as independent thinkers. Stop sheepishly following President Trump's line of reasoning; otherwise you will wake up in a dictatorship under the spell of his hypnosis.

President Trump is not a resourceful leader. Both cataclysmic occurrences present him with illimitable opportunities to put his leadership skills on display, but he has failed to take control and to lead. When that happens, the two other branches of government are to take over and address the wishes of the American people. The political, economic, and social experiment established by the United States Constitution in 1787 is currently at risk of failing. Failure to use the coronavirus pandemic and George Floyd's murder to bring about radical changes will ensure the total failure of that experiment.

In the case of the coronavirus pandemic, President Trump watched as the façade of his greatest economy on earth was blown away with astonishing speed, leaving Blacks, Hispanics and Native Americans and other minorities dying like flies. Where did the proceeds from the greatest economy go? Forty-plus million Americans filed for unemployment within a month of the manifestation of the coronavirus pandemic. Poor and middle-income Americans were joining food lines within three weeks of the nation's shutdown engendered by the coronavirus pandemic.

All Americans are spectators to these horrific and embarrassing episodes, but you lawmakers are not just spectators. The Constitution gives you the power to act. President Trump has done nothing to unite the nation. He stokes the flames of partisan politics to keep you divided so that he can rule. Unite and rise above this banal tactic for the sake of the American people and address the coronavirus pandemic. Override President Trump and follow the scientists out of this wilderness of death and destruction engendered by the coronavirus pandemic and an inept tyrant.

You must remember that when the framers wrote the Constitution, they expected Congress to keep the president in check. Congress has an obligation to protect the people. They were the people's elected officials. In writing the Constitution, the framers did not factor in political parties. Political parties were an unplanned feature of the democratic experiment. In the process of ratifying the Constitution, two political parties emerged. It is a testament to the framers' thoughtfulness and thoroughness that the new document was able to easily accommodate the Federalists and the Anti-Federalists, the first two political parties.

The history of political parties in the United States is documented elsewhere. The emergence of the two-party system, the Democrats and the Republicans, is what is critical at this juncture. Over time, these two parties have become extremely polarized to the extent that they can get very little done in Congress. Even more importantly, they have both lost the will to compromise and make laws in the people's interest. They are both focused on what is good for the party and the constituents they represent. That makes both parties vulnerable to control and manipulation by a corrupt president. Focus on the people nationwide and change your modus operandi. The coronavirus pandemic and George Floyd's murder are the signals that must not go unnoticed.

The current president, Donald J. Trump, demands 100 percent loyalty from members of his Republican Party. If a representative is not in lockstep with President Trump's policies, they are likely to be pushed out of the Republican Party. This was not the framers' intent. Congresspersons were expected to challenge the president when his policies were not in the best interest of the people. The current Congress is not using its oversight and override powers to good advantage. President Trump is dismantling the Constitution block by block with your help. In silence lies complicity.

For example, President Trump has completely modified the job description of the attorney general, who appears to be doing the president's bidding instead of looking out for the people's interest. Legal luminaries can articulate what is going on with the president's behavior regarding his demand that the court system drops cases against his friends and associates or lessens their sentences. He is violating the checks and balances principles of the Constitution by firing five inspectors general who were believed to be investigating the president or his associates, all within his first term of office. You need to put on your crack mender's robe and fix this emerging crack in the Constitution's democratic armor.

Lay citizens' objective view is that the president, the master builder that he is, is laying the foundation for something far more sinister. The American people have a right to know what the president is up to with these moves. If they are not told, then they are going to speculate.

Watching the president's behavior with dictators gives the impression that he is laying the foundation to remove the two-term clause of his tenure in order to serve indefinitely. His admired counterparts in Russia and Turkey have set precedents. His beloved

Kim Jung Un inherited a tradition of authoritarian rule. President Trump admires him a lot. The president's behavior toward Putin and his fascination with this dictator suggests that is the leader he wants to emulate. The American people are wondering if he is using Putin's playbook in extending the constitutional limits of his tenure. They are asking if President Trump's sojourn with Kim Jung Un was a mere distractor to take the focus off Putin.

One thing is certain, and that is President Trump has no interest in anything going on in this country except his second term in office. The coronavirus pandemic may have disrupted his sinister plan. This theory seems to explain his total inability to seize opportunities that present themselves to take the reins of the country, take control, and contain the coronavirus pandemic. He has also failed to seize the reins in the opportunity offered by George Floyd's murder and the Black Lives Matter marches on the streets of the United States, demanding an end to systemic racism and social inequalities.

The solutions to these problems cannot be the same old wishy-washy strategies used year in year out. First, the president's unconstitutional behaviors must be checked. You already have the tools to do that. Use them. Furthermore, you have to think outside the box this time. The greatest economy on earth should not have a single citizen dying for lack of health care. No American should be hungry in a calamity that did not spoil or destroy the nation's stockpiles of food. All Americans should be able to survive a calamity. Your European counterparts have put measures in place to do just that. When the Canadian and European economies were locked down, workers were assured of their wages and appropriate health care.

The United States' poor had to go back to work before it was safe to do so, thereby helping to spike the coronavirus pandemic's spread. You must put in place a living wage for all workers. There must be a national emergency fund that will not dry up at the first sign of a crisis. The nation's emergency fund must be given an inexhaustible character. In the greatest economy on earth, the majority of citizens should not have to be living paycheck to paycheck.

Andrew Yang, a candidate in the Democratic primary, had an intervention theory to provide $1,000 per month to the head of each household. Make Andrew Yang a consultant and investigate his proposal. If this proposal is not viable, you must come up with one of your own. So far, you have been poor stewards of the nation's resources. The American people deserve better. Your strategy of giving huge tax cuts to the 1 percent who do not need it must end. Five hundred billion dollars of the coronavirus relief package went to companies unknown, while thousands of small businesses have yet to receive any form of aid or loans.

President Trump's idea of asking the Supreme Court to overturn the Affordable Care Act in the midst of the coronavirus pandemic is callous. What is even worse, the Republican Party does not have an alternative plan. The American people deserve to have the same level of health care that congresspersons and the president have. The American taxpayers are the ones paying your health care bills, but you have a superior quality plan to the one the people have; some Americans have no health care whatsoever.

Bernie Sanders advanced a health care intervention theory during the Democratic primary. It looked far-fetched until the coronavirus pandemic struck. This is the type of health care coverage that is going to make sense in the future. The policies controlled by insurance companies who deny coverage at every opportunity should end. The nation's workforce should have the assurance that all their health care needs will be met regardless of whether or not they are employed. The need to take out a second mortgage to pay for health care procedures must come to an end. No American citizen should lose a dwelling because of health care issues. Until these issues are addressed and solved, the greatest economy on earth is a misnomer.

Americans also need to have the best education policy at all levels. Education, like health care, is a right. The coronavirus pandemic has disrupted the nation's education. Most of the nation's schools have been shut since the middle of March. The president has failed to take control and lead the nation. The CDC guidelines must be followed to reopen schools safely. The United States Congress must assume responsibilities in crisis situations. Congress needs to provide the appropriate funding to make sure that schools have the additional space, personnel, and testing supplies to safely open. Congress has to fill the gap and make sure the nation's education is not stultified during the coronavirus pandemic.

Congress, in the national interest, has the power to override President Trump's plan to force governors to reopen schools as usual and to cut funding if they don't. So far, not one of the 535 lawmakers has rebutted the president's threat to cut off school funding. A setback in education could negatively impact the nation for years to come. Moreover, education is a right, and no American citizen should be burdened with debt in order to get an education. The burden of all student loans should be removed, and future students should be educated by taxpayers' revenue to whatever level they qualify for. An educated workforce will redound to the benefit of the nation's political, economic, and social development. Wake up. Congress! The people are getting impatient. They see you as aiding and abetting the tyranny of political ignorance when you fail to assert your constitutional power and get on the side of the American people.

8
THE AMERICAN PEOPLE

Y ou are all the people who were referenced before. You are the educators, the businesspeople, the students, the police establishment, the professional organizations, the marchers on the streets, the civil rights activists, past and present, the congresspersons, the president, and all American citizens and others living and working here. You are America. Thomas Jefferson challenged you to work toward equality. Some of you have been equal from day one. Others of you have been an obstacle to equality from day one. Some of you were shut out of the equality paradigm, but you have fought your way in. Others of you have fought and have seen the promisedland, but you still have problems feeling that you are in. Some of you were murdered because of your struggles to be equal. There are no spectators here; you are all players in the long, drawn-out game of scavenger hunt for equality and justice.

Many of you have been warriors against the white supremacist movement. You have won some victories, and the demographics of the recent marches in response to George Floyd's murder offer a great deal of hope. The burgeoning tide of the new technologies and their abilities to capture the crimes as they are taking place is helping to flush out some of the enemies of equality. Education is also bringing the nation nearer to the equality goal. The mistake that could reverse the gains made is complacency. There is no room for complacency. The white supremacists have friends in high places. The people, all of them, must remain vigilant. Some of you must learn from your children, who have interacted with peers of all races, ethnicities, and religions in the nation's public schools and have found them to be quite similar in most ways. The myth that minorities are dangerous is blown by children in public schools. Students have proven at all levels of society that all minorities are capable of reaching the highest goals if the hurdles in their way are taken down.

All of you were seen on the streets of America protesting for justice and equality. Some of you were there in spirit, and your presence was felt. Others of you did your share of protests in the past and can only inspire young spectators now. You can be proud though, for the seeds you sowed fell on fertile soil and have sprung up and are growing lustily. In the crops of the future lies the hope of equality. Do not be alarmed when the results do not come with a click of the mouse. Some have grown used to the instant gratification syndrome, but the seekers of equality know to wait a bit more. You must be in control of the time variable though.

This means you have the weapon in hand, the vote. Do some serious thinking and evaluate your present standing. Calculate the distance very carefully and pick the right targets. Elect the right people with a mandate to get your demands met. Do not ever allow complacency to take root. Keep up the relentless pressure of protests, like the ones seen on the streets all over the United States in recent times. Feed on the energy of those protests and fight until the last obstacle is removed.

Remember that getting the laws on the books is but a beginning. You and your children are going to have to work to give the laws teeth. Sometimes there is a tendency to leave things up to the law. That does not always work. You are going to have to cultivate vigilance and practice it at every level of the journey. Yes, it is possible to view the promisedland and be unable to enter. That happens when there is lack of preparation and premature declaration of victory.

Victory will come when your Black sons and daughters are safe in their goings out and comings in. When you find that you do not have to teach your sons how to behave when they encounter a police officer, you will know changes are coming. You will taste victory when your sons and daughters consistently relate civil encounters with police officers. Change will come when police officers are penalized for slamming suspects to the ground even though they did not resist arrest. Police officers will show courtesy to all people, and you can tell that they are not pretending. You may have to wait for the old guard to change and use vigilance to keep the new ones in check.

Law enforcement officers will begin to have human faces as an outcome of additional training and retooling. Members of the law enforcement establishments, through education and supervision, will begin to focus on citizens' safety first and eliminate brute force as a strategy of apprehension. The police will show maturity and deescalate even egregious and dangerous situations. Victory will be at hand when all police and suspects' encounters are automatically recorded and later reviewed by a neutral authority. Police officers who write reports that are not in alignment with the findings of the neutral authority are removed from the force.

You will know that your efforts are bearing fruits when there is no longer one set of laws for police officers and another set for everyone else. There will be just one law for all. Gradually, the fear you normally have when a police officer approaches your person, your home, or vehicle will begin to dissipate. When most police/citizens' encounters end with respect and understanding, these will be the signs of changing times. Do not expect all of these to happen simultaneously. Remember that gradualism is a potent force and that you are not to rush change. Instead, make sure your generation does all in its power and prepare the next generation to carry the baton to the next post.

You will know that the equality goals are being addressed when you begin to see evidence that the progressive taxation system is focused on low-income families and the vulnerable populations. Additionally, there will be obvious signs that health care plans are programmed to examine the plight of the vulnerable populations. There will be clear signals that educations curricula are aligned to the academic achievement of all students. You will know that the equality goals are being met when you begin to see people who look like yourself in all segments of the business hierarchy and in public establishments.

Look out for the following signs as a result of the devastation caused by the coronavirus pandemic and the national embarrassment as a result of the George Floyd's murder. Businesses will learn that they lose when they shut out qualified individuals because of the color, gender, religion, and sexual preferences. The business boycott weapon becomes a potent force with the promise of improvement day by day. You will observe the businesses themselves using the boycott weapon against establishments that operate outside the norm and are patently bigoted. Keep your focus on where big businesses put their advertisement dollars and sponsorships. Corporate citizenship can do as much to remove the social inequalities that permeate the society as the government can. You will see businesses stepping up to the plate to eradicate the existing student loan burden and join with the government in making sure that poverty is not an inhibitor to the highest educational achievement. You will observe businesses finding or cultivating a moral compass, which will make them do less tax evasion and fewer loophole searches. Instead, businesses will begin to carry their fair share of the work of removing the social inequalities that place some groups permanently at the bottom of the social and economic ladder. You are going to be singing that old song that explains that these changes have been a long time coming. Keep on singing and hoping and doing. Vigilance must never abate, for that is when abuse will creep in and clog the wheels of change. It is always the people who overcome tyranny, no matter the form it takes.

To those of you who are white, please note that you are not lumped in the white supremacist class. Most white people are ordinary, fair-minded individuals who believe in equal opportunities for all. Blacks have never fought alone. At every step of the road to equality, white people have given blacks a helping hand. Many whites believed in the equality paradigm from day one and confronted slavery from its inception. They featured in the many movements and strategies that the slaves used to escape bondage. Some whites were prominent abolitionists who fought with the movement and led the way to emancipation with their blood and treasure.

They were part of the Freedom Riders, a movement to pressure the South to end Jim Crow laws. An all-white Supreme Court voted unanimously to end segregation in public schools. Furthermore, many whites marched with the Reverend Dr. Martin Luther King and got the Civil Rights Bill and the Voting Rights Act through the United States Congress. Many whites in both Houses of Congress have been champions of the struggles for blacks and minority progress. The demographic diversity in the Black Lives Matter marches engendered by George Floyd's brutal murder was not created overnight. It is the accumulation of years of support, through love, mutual respect, intermarriage, schooling, athletics, music, arts, and a host of other human interactions. A salute to all the whites who have been part of the struggle for equality and justice for blacks and minorities in the United States. America will not know true equality until all groups are equal. That way, they will not allow the tyranny of political ignorance to go on indefinitely. They have the vote to make the difference.

9

PRESIDENT TRUMP'S "INDEPENDENCE" SPEECH 2020

The main focus of President Trump's "Independence" speech delivered from Mount Rushmore was breathing life into the United States' monuments and statues. He did this while the death count from the coronavirus pandemic was approaching 130,000 and almost three million Americans were infected with the disease. Many of the infected face lifelong impairments from this disease. In his "Independence" speech, President Trump managed to reference the coronavirus disease, this invisible engine of silent destruction, just once. Only an insane genius could accomplish a feat such as this. No one but an insane genius could motivate thousands of supporters to attend a rally and expose themselves to the coronavirus disease in an environment where there was no social distancing and wearing a mask was not mandatory. Most supporters at this gathering wore no masks. This scenario conjures up images of previous cult leaders who had sinister motives.

Additionally, in his "Independence" address, President Trump saw hate in the Black Lives Matter marches. You can only see hate in this movement if you are an insane genius. Black Lives Matter emanates from a place where black people were enslaved, stripped of their dignity and their humanity. Blacks were not allowed to own property. They were not allowed to learn to read. They learned the English language without formal classes. Yet they were ridiculed for the way they spoke, for the way they dressed, and the way they looked. The process of indoctrination they experienced forced them to accept that they were an inferior people. Worse still, they had to acknowledge that the whites were a superior race. This is the birth of racial bias. Even blacks came to believe that white is good and black is bad. Many blacks are still in a state of mental slavery. Moreover, white supremacist slave owners held the power of life or death over them. They could be sold without their consent because they were property. Their children were often sold without parents' knowledge. Grief for the loss of their children is embedded in the souls of African American mothers in all their sojourn in this land.

Blacks survived slavery and its dehumanizing tentacles for 256 years only to face Jim Crow laws in the southern United States after emancipation. Under Jim Crow laws, lynching the black man was as frequent as breathing. Jim Crow laws effectively established an apartheid system in which housing, schooling, transportation, and other facilities had to be separate. Blacks were forced to endure the inferior portions in all facets of live. Law enforcement turned a blind eye as the white supremacist Ku Klux Klan wreaked havoc on black people's attempt to learn how to live as free people, to read, to vote, and to own property.

The struggles for black people to be other than what the white supremacists made them has been one of humanity's longest and most humiliating experiences. The slave patrols under slavery morphed into the law enforcement establishment during Jim Crow laws. During slavery, the slave patrols had an obligation to return the slave alive because he was the white supremacist's property. For many blacks, emancipation meant giving their lives for freedom. Law enforcement's licenses to kill coincided with the emancipation of the slaves.

The enlightened views of President Truman in the late 1940s brought about desegregation of the military and triggered changes that culminated in the Supreme Court's intervention to desegregate transportation and public facilities. Later in 1954, in the landmark case

Brown v. Board of Education, the Supreme Court desegregated public school education. The civil rights movement brought some relief, but the majority of blacks are still facing the onslaught of political, economic, and social inequalities. The majority of blacks are still on the lowest rungs of the political, economic, and social stratification ladder. Racial bias permeates the justice system that disproportionately imprisons blacks. Black suspects are three and a half times more likely than their white counterparts to be killed in police encounters. Blacks represent about 13 percent of the United States population but over 40 percent of the prison population.

The Black Lives Matter movement is simply an attempt to bring to light that all of the United States' history has been an effort to treat black people as if they are invisible, as if they are not there. Law enforcement certainly feels that way. To strengthen the invisible perception, recently, two United States senators posting tributes to John Lewis on his passing had Elijah Cummings pictured in the post. Both Representatives were senior colleagues of the two senators for years. That these senators were not able to differentiate between the two black representatives speaks volume to the Black Lives Matter statement.

Many police officers make the point even more poignantly. Recently, white police officers in Colorado killed a black young man and reenacted the killing as a form of entertainment. Police officers kneel on black people's necks, relaxed, with hand in pocket while the victims beg for air and die calling for their mothers. It has to be an overpowering sense of racial bias that leads a sitting United States president to see hate in the current Black Lives Matter protests. The Black Lives Matter movement is simply asking that blacks be respected and recognized as human beings.

At the Mount Rushmore rally, President Trump also accused teachers of indoctrinating students. The insane genius does not read history. He has admitted that he does not read books. He is a visual learner. Teachers put the spotlight on the events of history. They do not create the events. White supremacists in the South wanted to hold African Americans as slaves in perpetuity. White supremacist states seceded from the Union to fight for the right to keep slaves forever. Secession from the Union was treason. White supremacist generals were defeated in the Civil War. Blacks in these states have to put up with all the discrimination, abuse, racism, lynching, and all manner of atrocities, including looking at the statues of these white supremacists who have tormented them for centuries. The history is what it is, President Trump.

Racial bias drove President Andrew Jackson to violate the law when he disobeyed the Supreme Court and moved the Native Americans from Georgia to Oklahoma. The Native Americans died in great numbers on that journey. To the Native Americans, the journey was the Trails of Tears. Some historians equate the Trail of Tears with genocide. Tearing down those statues is a form of symbolic speech. Putting them up was not.

President Trump watched the murder of George Floyd and expressed concern, but there was no heart in it. When a journalist asked President Trump how he feels about blacks being killed by police, his racial bias surged to the fore, evoking the response, "Whites are dying too, more whites than blacks." He then berated the journalist for asking a terrible question. President Trump watched the streets of the United States fill up with marchers supporting the Black Life Matter movement. He saw only thugs marching on the streets of the United States. The marchers were a mix of all Americans, blacks, whites, Hispanics, Native Americans, Asians, and others. The murder of George Floyd and the marchers on the streets supporting the Black Lives Matter movement taught Americans more than any teacher could in a lifetime.

Mr. President, you should have learned something too, but it is obvious that you did not. If you were a genius in the positive sense of the word, you would have realized that it was a moment for you to take control and unite the American people. Neither blacks nor whites should be killed by the police establishment at the rate that it is occurring in this country. All of President Trump's actions to date point to dividing the nation. It must be admitted that he is great at what he does. History, and not teachers, will record him as the "divider in chief."

President Trump, you owe all teachers an apology. The fact that it is not forthcoming does not negate it. You owe them an apology. They do not indoctrinate students. They teach with all of their being. They are professionals who are committed to the ideals and values of the United States. They are mostly underpaid and undervalued. Most of them have to use the sparse income they make to supplement the grossly inadequate school supplies in your greatest economy on earth. Teachers are the only caregivers many students have. Teachers have to play the role of parent, nurse, detective, provider, babysitter, and more. The coronavirus pandemic blew the façade off your great economy, leaving many parents begging for schools to reopen so that the teacher/babysitter can help them to go back to work. Your great economy uses teachers as babysitters, but you do not pay them for that service. How dare you accuse them of indoctrinating students?

On a different note, interpretation of the Second Amendment may turn out to be one of the greatest cracks in the United States' democratic armor. James Madison would be horrified if he could observe the power of the National Rifle Association today. Madison conceptualized a government in which no one minority group could control the government, as the majority would override the single group. He grossly underestimated the power of the Second Amendment in the hands of people who care more about profit than the sanctity of human lives.

The National Rifle Association virtually controls the government in the United States today. It does not run for office directly, but it has most of those who do leaning on it for funding for their campaign. Politicians who oppose the National Rifle Association run the risk of having the organization finance their opponent's campaign. In a nation where money usually makes the difference between who wins and who loses an election, it is suicidal to go against the NRA in a serious contest. It is rumored that the National Rifle Association wrote the Stand Your Ground Law in the state of Florida and handed it to the lawmakers, who had no option but to steer it through the legislative process.

America is the most dangerous place for anyone to live right now, the coronavirus pandemic aside. The nation is not at war on American soil, but yearly, its death toll by the gun far outnumbers that of many countries that are experiencing war. Sebastian Murdock claims that more people have died by the gun in the United States since 1963 than have died in all the wars the United States has engaged in combined.

10

CONFRONTING THE PRESIDENT'S POLITICAL IGNORANCE

M r. President, many Americans believe that under your tenure, the nation is experiencing the tyranny of political ignorance. This is mostly your own fault. It is your duty to have your fingers on the pulse of the nation at all times. The office of the presidency is not one of self. It is all about the people of the United States and their most urgent needs. Right at this moment, there are two cataclysmic crises before the nation in the form of the coronavirus pandemic and the gruesome police murder of George Floyd beamed on national television. Both require the president to take control and set agendas for solutions.

In the case of the coronavirus, your first task is to get the Centers for Disease Control (CDC) to set some parameters for the nation to follow to overcome this pandemic. You are not a scientist, so you cannot inject yourself and your thinking in the parameters. The office of the presidency carries a great deal of respect. It is not you who the American people respect; it is the office. It does not matter who is in the office. If you want the people's respect personally, you must earn it. You do that by directing and assuring the American people at all times.

Mr. President, you have an obligation to present the CDC guidelines in a solemn tone and not to deviate from them in any way. In doing this, it may clash with some of your personal goals, but because it is the people's health first, you have to forgo your personal goals. You have to be a very strong leader to do that. If you do otherwise, you send mixed signals to the American people, and the CDC guidelines get muddled up. It calls for a lot of restraint to put yourself in the background when you are the president of the United States. Another way to look at it is that you are still in the forefront when the CDC is operating, for the CDC is one of the agencies you control. The American people know this, Mr. President.

You also need to take control at the national level. Under the Articles of Confederation, the United States' first constitution, there was no president, and the states could not manage crises at the national level. The Constitution you are under currently created the office of the president to address national issues. You had a lot of problems taking control of the coronavirus pandemic. Failure to take control takes the nation back to the years leading up to 1787. That is very poor performance, Mr. President. It is a blatant case of aggravated neglect.

Your son-in-law and adviser lay claim to hospital resources in the statement that "they are ours," meaning the federal government and not the states own the health supplies in question. This is ignorance on steroids. The resources are the peoples.' The president in crises mode controls all the people's resources and makes sure all fifty states have adequate supplies. The states must inform you of their needs, but they are not really begging you for anything, Mr. President. The "woman from Michigan" did not have to treat you "nice" or any other way. As governor, it is her responsibility to inform you what the state of Michigan needs. She is doing her duty as governor. Even if she had been impolite, and she was not, you would be duty bound to supply the states' needs in the coronavirus pandemic crisis. You can't be petty and be president. The Constitution gives you the power to call up the National Guard and the Army Corps of Engineers to assist you to take control and manage the nation in crisis. Use them appropriately.

Your urging the nation back to work, violating the CDC guidelines, was not presidential. You have to learn to follow the scientists. Logical thinking would have brought you to the place where you see that people's lives are more important than the economy. It is hard to come to grips with this, but it is true. Sick workers cannot run an economy effectively. Be patient, get the coronavirus under control, and then open up the economy and continue to motivate the American people to follow the CDC protocols. Eventually, the economy will recover, and you will have a healthy set of workers and a robust economy. Lead from the front, Mr. President, and model patience for the American people. Your leadership skills on display before the nation would be just as good as a recovered economy to ensure your second term. You could lose all if you fail to lead when it matters most.

You have to be an insane genius to want to send the students back to school when the coronavirus pandemic is peaking and the death rate is still climbing. Think this through carefully, Mr. President. You claim the students have a very powerful resistance to the coronavirus. However, they cannot teach themselves. Many people who are predisposed to the disease by age and by medical conditions must interact with students on a daily basis. They are vulnerable to the disease. Moreover, the students, their teachers, and other support personnel have to go home to elderly parents and members of their families, who may have underlying issues that make them predisposed to the coronavirus disease. You do not learn from prior mistakes, Mr. President. You instigated an early return to opening up the economy before the CDC guidelines indicated that it was safe to do so. The coronavirus disease curve was flattening at that time. The early opening of the economy created the current uncontrollable spike. Now you are recommending going back to school for all five days per week. This makes you appear both ignorant and heartless.

You are encouraging the coronavirus pandemic to explode irretrievably. Those countries in the European Union that you cited that are opening up their schools have flattened the curve, Mr. President. They have done that because they have real leaders who followed the scientists and motivated their people to be disciplined. You do not have those levels of leadership acumen. Furthermore, you do not seek to unite the people and foster good discipline. Every word out of your mouth divides the American people. You therefore have to be patient and make the CDC do its work. Wear a mask, Mr. President, and encourage all Americans to wear a mask and bring down the positive rate before you recommend opening up the schools.

Regarding the testing, no one but you can understand your logic. The goal should be to have every American tested. That way, you would know how to treat those with the coronavirus disease and keep the ones who are negative protected. By not testing everyone, there are bound to be people who have the disease and are continuously spreading it. You will only have control when testing reaches a level that indicates that fewer and fewer people are testing positive. Even then, you will have to continue testing until there are no positives whatsoever. Let the CDC do its work while you put plans in place to move the nation forward. So far, you tweet and speak a great deal of garbage, but the American people have no plan that you have generated as president and the leader of the greatest nation on earth.

Being a great president involves doing a lot that you do not agree with in the interest of the American people. For whatever reason you do not like a mask, wear it for the sake of the American people. Your CDC experts find that wearing a mask is the best way to protect the population. The CDC is your house, and you are the boss. If a house is divided against itself, it is going to fall, and you are going to pay the penalty because the nation is expecting you to guide the people out of the coronavirus pandemic. The new spike in the coronavirus pandemic in most of the states is your fault—failure to wear the mask and impatience in opening up the economy as directed by the CDC, your own agency.

You now have a second chance to fix the coronavirus pandemic. Put on the mask and apologize to the American people. Nobody is more forgiving than the American people. Follow the CDC protocols without fail and motivate all of Congress and the American people to do the same. You would be surprised at the results. The coronavirus pandemic would peak and genuinely flatten, and your economy would take off again. If you fail to follow these steps, the American people will wait out the rest of this year and give someone else the mandate to eradicate the coronavirus pandemic.

On the issue of the George Floyd tragedy, you made a lot of blunders. It is obvious that you have an affinity for the police establishment. However, you are the president of all the people. You cannot single out segments for special treatment. You will lose all the rest. There is a way to respect the police establishment and all the rest of the United States population. Just be impartial. Show concern for all the people's problems. Genuine sympathy should have flowed for George Floyd's family from you, your family, and from the United States people. You are the voice of the United States people. Take note of the word *genuine*. It is not just saying the words. It is how the American people hear the words coming out. They know when it is from your lips and not from your heart. You have not been able to get the heart in for George Floyd and for those who died in the coronavirus pandemic.

You should have gone to Minneapolis to comfort the people there. The murder on national television was gruesome. When it suits you, you have brought family members to the White House and to other gatherings. This was an occasion that warranted that type of invitation and comforting. All of America saw the murder and took to the streets. You labeled them thugs. That was not presidential. You are the president of all of America. You should have had the same emotions as all Americans. You were not to put the feeling of Donald J. Trump the man in the forefront. Yes, there were a few thugs, but the 330 million Americans were hurting. The people needed a comforter at that moment. You failed to comfort the American people at a critical moment.

You can redeem yourself if you stop thinking of yourself for a moment. You can tell the Congress of the United States that you need a bill on your desk that addresses the issues that the people on the streets are calling for. It is not about what Donald J. Trump is calling for. It is not about you, Mr. President. It is about the American people. The people want the police establishment reformed so that the killing of black people can stop. Both House Republicans and Senate Republicans fear you because they are weak and have given up their coequal power status in the checks and balances apparatus of the Constitution. Send the signal that you must have a bill on your desk, and the cowering Republicans will find the will to do your bidding. Again, you can follow this bit of advice, but knowing you, it is going to be difficult. However, if you don't, the people will replace you with a mandate to get their demands met.

11

THE LONG ROAD TO
THE PRESENT

Much has been done by the United States government and the American people to address the first crack that appeared in the nation's democratic armor. This first crack was the presence of slavery in the nation that held up the banner of freedom as its most prominent emblem. The cost in American blood and treasure to bring an end to slavery was horrendous. Almost seven hundred thousand lives were lost, and the southern economy was devastated.

The federal government's attempt to reconstruct the South, while well intentioned, did not have an opportunity to achieve its full potential. The resurgent South was able to push back on the constitutional protections of the former slaves, causing the Reconstruction efforts to subside without achieving most of its goals. However, under Reconstruction, African American slaves were emancipated in the aftermath of the Civil War. The Thirteenth Amendment outlawed slavery on United States soil in all forms forever. The Fourteenth Amendment granted citizenship to African Americans and gave them equal protection under the Constitution. Black males were allowed the right to vote in the Fifteenth Amendment.

Equal protection under the Constitution was on paper only. African Americans then and now still struggle to be treated fairly under the law. In the years following the Fourteenth Amendment, blacks were not allowed to serve as jurors. This meant the jury panels were all white in cases involving African Americans defendants. Because they were denied an education during slavery, blacks were not qualified to participate in the legal process at any level. They were disproportionately imprisoned for nonviolent crimes and usually received stiffer penalties than their white counterparts. During this period, the unlawful lynching of blacks was quite common, as the law enforcement establishment turned a blind eye.

Under Reconstruction, there was a brief period when African Americans participated in the political process and won seats in the governments at the local, state, and national levels. However, this was short-lived. As soon as Reconstruction ended, it became nearly impossible for African American males to vote, much less to run for office. In fact, many African Americans were lynched for attempting to cast a vote. Additionally, Jim Crow laws placed obstacles in the way of black male voters. They had to pass a literacy test, and they also had to pay a poll tax. It must also be remembered that not all African Americans were slaves. There were some free African Americans, but they too were restricted by state laws. Some states blocked interracial marriages and denied blacks the right to serve in most professions.

African Americans experienced many hardships under Jim Crow laws, which was effectively apartheid government. White supremacist governments in southern states mandated separate housing, separate schools, and public facilities. There were distinct differences between the superior white facilities and those reserved for African Americans. African Americans had to ride at the back of the bus or train, and they had to yield their seats to whites if the bus was overcrowded. The landmark case *Plessy v. Ferguson* legalized the Jim Crow law practice of separate but equal. Blacks were denied credit and opportunities to develop businesses. Moreover, black initiatives were ostracized by whites who refused to buy products that were made by African Americans. This level of neglect forced many African Americans to move to the north and west in search of better opportunities.

Many African Americans served in World War I in defense of American values but returned to the United States to face the same levels of segregation and discrimination. African Americans had to fight their way into the United States armed services. They have fought in every war that the United States has ever been involved in. They faced discrimination in every one of these wars until President Truman desegregated the military in 1948. The desegregation of the military set a precedent for the desegregation of public transportation, public facilities, and public schools. The Civil Rights Act of 1964 and the Voting Rights Act of 1965 have brought about changes that helped to bring African Americans closer to achieving the equality goals embedded in the Declaration of Independence, but there is much work to be done.

As a result of the Civil Rights Act of 1964 and the Voting Rights Act of 1965, many new developments are observable today. Minorities are now qualified to serve at all levels of the nation's private and public sectors. Prior to these political achievements, these groups were mostly unrepresented in these fields. Progress that can be directly attributed to the Civil Rights Act of 1964 manifested itself in the election of Barack Obama, the first black president of the United States in 2008. Most minority children can now aspire to reach lofty goals. As a result of the Voting Rights Act of 1965, 116 minority representatives now serve in the 116th Congress. This is a new record, representing very favorable outcomes of the civil rights movement. It also suggests that blacks are inching toward the equality goals of the Declaration of Independence and helping to mend the first crack in the United States' democratic armor.

A lot of work is needed to address political, economic, and social inequalities that are the direct result of systemic racism. The Black Lives Matter marches, in protest of George Floyd's killing, reflect a very high mix of the nation's demographics demanding these changes. This demographic mix offers hope that future generations of lawmakers are not going to tolerate the high levels of inequity that they see around them today. They also are dissatisfied with the high levels of police brutality targeting black people, and they want the government to address this issue immediately. Government is on notice to act promptly or be ousted in favor of a replacement with a mandate to act.

Regarding the issue of political ignorance as a serious crack in the nation's democratic armor, it is reasonable to deduce from the marches on the streets of America, protesting the murder of George Floyd that changes are coming. The protestors on the streets are signaling that they are about to use the available information to bring about societal changes. What is even more important is that the marchers themselves are recommending the changes they would like to see. Some of these changes may be too drastic and out of line, but at least they are getting the attention of Congress, the president, and all Americans. When lawmakers are pressured to the point of annoyance, they sometimes wake up and do the work they were elected to do in the first place. The Black Lives Mater marchers have been tormenting lawmakers, and it is hoped that some changes will emanate from this pressure.

The signals coming from the marchers also reinforce the suggestion that there should be a congressional effort to educate the population to make citizens genuinely knowledgeable about the history and functions of the nation's political, economic, and social institutions. The recommended revivalist movement would get the entire nation prepared and ready to identify anomalies in the system and take the necessary measures to address them before they reach crisis proportions, as evidenced by the George Floyd killing. The revivalist movement would be sneering many birds with a single stone. The nation would be receiving a sound education foundation on the history and development of the political process and at the same time preparing knowledgeable leaders to take the reins of the country in the future. This education with the attendant incentives would extend beyond schools into the general population, with no age restrictions.

Businesses would become involved and more aware of their role in promoting a moral and ethical society. The movement would awaken the conscience of the nation and compel everyone to take stock of their role in removing the inequities that make the nation appear so imbalanced in times of crisis. It would make the entire nation less resistant to change, as all groups would come to realize that injustice to one group is injustice to all groups and that all forms of injustice inhibit the nation's progress. No chain is stronger than its weakest link. Puerto Rico is a part of the United States. If it is poor and weak, the United States bears a level of responsibility for this situation. No United States president has the right to denigrate any part of the United States. A president's role is to uplift, to see paths of light that will guide the nation out of its problems. Puerto Rico's problems are the United States' problems, and the United States' problems must be addressed by the United States' government.

Furthermore, a revivalist movement focused on the role of government and the responsibilities of the citizenry in the political process would help to create the feeling that all Americans are critically important in the decision-making processes that drive the nation's development. The movement would create a whole army of new leaders ready to assume responsibility and address the nation's shortcomings. An informed electorate would be created that would help to guide leadership in ways that are not confrontational and destructive. The population would move closer to the concept that the nation is truly one people and pressure its lawmakers to be less partisan and work for the promotion of the entire nation instead of the pervasive interest-group syndrome that dominates the society presently.

Lack of political knowledge is responsible for the high levels of complacency that permeate society presently. Interest groups lobby Congress and get away with all manner of atrocities, while the politically ignorant populace sits back and does nothing under the fallacious assumption that this is the way politics works. Politics works this way when citizens are not aware and do not know how to challenge lobbyists and their narrow, partisan views. An educated populace knows how to push back by electing those representatives who will respect the wishes of the people. A politically astute citizenry knows how to be vigilant without being offensive. They know how to bring shady deals into the open and embarrass the perpetrator of crimes against the American people. Perpetrators of crimes, at all levels, deserve to be imprisoned.

Educating the public is critical because the world gets more complex every day. An uneducated populace finds it difficult to understand some of the complex statistics that are displayed before them every day. The intricacies of modern economics confounds even the highly educated. It requires specialists in every branch of economics to explain how systems work. The same is true of law, medicine, and a host of other disciplines that impact daily lives. The world today revolves around specialization. The population has to be on the cutting edge of the new technologies to be able to keep up in any field, especially the field of politics.

Understanding politics on the home front is one thing. In a global economy, international politics and international relations are just as critical. Understanding the dynamics of globalism is just as critical as understanding the nation's economic and political day-to-day functions. The uneducated today are at the mercy of those who would seek to exploit them. To survive in today's political and economic environments, all citizens need to be knowledgeable about what is going on in all parts of the world. Education helps the population to find alternatives and more efficient strategies to cope. Participation in the political process can be beneficial materially and intellectually. Political education brings out the awareness that if citizens are not participating in the political process, they are not getting all that they are entitled to.

The political ignorance of President Donald J. Trump is a multidimensional issue. Just being an ignorant president poses a risk to the United States' democracy. It is appalling that candidate Trump displayed the level of political ignorance that he did and still won the presidency. It is an indictment on the American electorate. It is an indictment on all Americans because the nation's political system is premised on the majoritarian formula. Once candidate Trump won the 2016 election, he became the president of the United States and all its citizens. On this premise, his election is an indictment on all of the citizens. It is reasonable to argue that the electorate expected candidate Trump to change his brash and disdainful attitude once he became the president of the United States and behave in a manner befitting that high office.

However, voters are appalled to find that there is just one Donald Trump, politically ignorant, disrespectful of all people and especially women, immoral, unethical, arrogant, egotistical, inept, and incorrigible. Moreover, Donald Trump lacks leadership qualities at all levels. He was reputed to be the most bankrupt businessman in the country, judging by the number of times he declared bankruptcy. It should have been palpably obvious that he was going to be bankrupt in leadership qualities and solutions when crisis struck, but the electorate failed to grasp that connection. Finally, Donald Trump lacks empathy and the ability to follow simple instructions. The insane genius never apologizes and never, ever accepts responsibility.

President Trump's political ignorance presents a crack in the United States' democratic armor. His occupation of that high office will present other cracks in geometric progression. For example, he immediately demonstrated to the nation, on assuming the presidency, what he thought the attorney general should be to himself as president—his personal watchdog. The attorney general, when the office was conceptualized, would advise the president on the affairs of the people. President Trump threw tantrums when his first attorney general, Jeff Sessions, recused himself and refused to do his biddings in the Muller investigation.

President Trump subsequently put out feelers for a puppet attorney general. William Barr applied for and got the job. In that one appointment, innumerable cracks have opened up in the United States' democratic armor. William Barr read the Muller Report upside down to give the appearance that candidate Donald Trump did not collude with the Russians in the 2016 presidential election. President Trump's attorney general, William Barr, has gone on to engage in numerous behaviors that are not within the bounds of his job description. He has effectively become President Trump's legal adviser, and he has engaged in activities that are going to create precedents for future presidents if the United States make it thus far.

Additionally, President Trump's political ignorance leads him to violate the rule of law knowingly and unknowingly. His egotistical trait makes him very impatient in following routines. For example, the court procedures frustrate him. He wants to issue orders and have them frozen in law as he speaks or writes. When these are referred to the courts in the checks and balances procedures, he is totally frustrated. He denigrates justices who rule against his illegal executive orders.

All that was normal before President Trump has now become abnormal. It is a norm for presidential candidates since the 1970s to declare their tax returns for review. Candidate Trump refused to submit his tax returns, and the United States electorate allowed him to get away with it. He claimed absolute immunity from investigation as president, but the Supreme Court did not agree with him in this regard, and his bank accounts will be reviewed by the prosecutors in the Southern District Court of New York at some future date. The president of the United States is under investigation by the Southern District of New York for campaign finance violations and other charges.

Moreover, President Trump violated the Constitution by asking foreign powers to help him win elections against his opponents. He publicly claimed that he would be willing to accept negative reports on his opponents from foreign powers. What is even more alarming is that President Trump was impeached for soliciting help from the Ukrainian president to open an investigation into his pending opponent's son. However, his Republican supporters in the House of Representatives found nothing wrong with that. The Senate subsequently acquitted President Trump on the impeachment charge of abuse of power. The Senate majority leader publicly announced that he would not be impartial in his review of the evidence. Other Republican Senators also claimed that they would not be impartial. The cracks in the democratic armor keep widening. The impeachment process created several other cracks in the United States' democratic armor.

Other cracks in the democratic armor were contingent on President Trump's exoneration in his impeachment trial. President Trump fired all the people who did their constitutional duties because they reported his inappropriate behaviors and testified before Congress, as they were legally bound to do. Additionally, President Trump opened more cracks in the democratic armor when he fired all the inspectors general investigating his unconstitutional behaviors. More cracks are being opened as the president seeks to have the courts drop cases against his associates and friends or lessen their punishment.

James Madison thought it was not necessary to put limits on the president's power to pardon, arguing that if the president pardoned his friends, Congress would immediately impeach him. Madison would rotate in his grave if he were able to watch President Trump's abuse of his pardon powers. The idea of impeaching the president for pardoning his friends and associates is not forthcoming. The same Congress that exonerated him on his first impeachment charge of abuse of power is still sitting. The partisan divide makes this an absolute waste of time. Congress's only recourse at the moment is to propose an amendment to the Constitution to limit a president's ability to use the presidential pardon for friends and associates. Whether or not this amendment will successfully go through the amendment procedures is another matter.

Political parties were not contemplated at the Constitutional Convention in 1787. They emerged as an unplanned feature of the ratification process. The Constitution was able to accommodate them without problems. In recent times, however, political parties have started to present themselves as a challenge to the United States' democracy. They have become polarized and almost incapable of effectively managing the nation's affairs. Many of the ills that face the nation have been in gridlock for many years. For example, administration after administration has watched the nation's infrastructure crumbling. Both parties see the need for action to be taken to fix the problem, but so far nothing has happened. A similar situation exists with the nation's health care. One party passed the Affordable Care Act, and the other party has been fighting tooth and nail to dismantle it, even though it has never been able to offer a viable alternative. Democracy has the reputation for presenting difficulties in getting laws passed. The two-party system in the United States has taken this reputation to an almost uncontrollable dimension.

After World War II, Russia (Soviet Union) and the United States achieved superpower statuses on either side of the capitalist/communist divide. Russia has since become the United States' number one geopolitical adversary. There might have been a lull in their adversarial animosity during President Regan's tenure and the subsequent collapse of the Soviet Union. A resurgent Russia is jealous of the United States' sole superpower status. It is on a mission focused on territorial aggrandizement, which led to the capture of Crimea, a part of Ukraine, a violation of international law. Ukraine is an ally of the United States.

Instead of standing up to Russia as other United States presidents have done, President Donald Trump insists on having a personal, friendly relationship with Russia's president, Vladimir Putin. A crack in the democratic armor was created when President Trump, at a Helsinki meeting, took the word of President Putin over that of his own intelligence agencies. This was beamed on international television. President Trump's behavior in this and other issues has raised all sorts of questions about the United States' national security. It also raised speculation that President Trump is beholden to Vladimir Putin, the Russian president, in some strange way.

President Trump's political ignorance led him to forgo standard operating procedures and initiate meetings between himself and Kim Jung Un, the North Korean president. In this scenario, his egotistical trait surged to the fore. The idea that he and he alone can get it done replaced the nation's age-old strategies in international diplomacy. The president has achieved nothing in these meetings, and it is rumored that North Korea has since doubled its nuclear stockpile, the very goal that President Trump's meetings should have prevented. Standard operating procedures would have had skilled negotiators from the State Department lay the foundation for a meeting with Kim Jung Un and the United States president. All the groundwork would have been laid and the conditions of the meetings determined.

These procedures give the United States president the option to proceed or not to proceed with the high-level meeting, based on the content of the agenda. President Trump's penchant for his personal style of wishy-washy diplomacy sets a precedent. Future leaders may want to meet with the United States president without predetermined conditions and waste the nation's time and resources. It also confers a false sense of power status on the other player in the process. Moreover, it diminishes the United States' power status.

The United States lost a great deal of international respect when President Trump unadvisedly pulled the United States forces out of Syria and left the Kurds exposed to Turkey's military might. President Trump appears to be beholden to the Turkish President too in some strange way. This move also pleased Vladimir Putin. These Kurdish fighters were very instrumental in driving the terrorist organization ISIS out of Syria and Iraq. They were critical allies of the United States. The unceremonious manner in which President Trump abandoned them and left them to be slaughtered by the Turks has done nothing to promote the United States as a champion of democracy on the international scene. This behavior will create a stumbling block in building future alliances. It will create a trust issue in times of international crises.

The collision of the coronavirus pandemic and the police murder of George Floyd on the streets of Minneapolis exposed some cracks in the United States' democratic armor and created others. The coronavirus removed the façade from the United States' distribution of scarce resources. With unflappable consistency, blacks and minorities were found at the bottom of the scarce resources distribution scale. They were disproportionately affected by the coronavirus pandemic both in the infection and death rate. This was clear and convincing evidence that systemic racism is pervasive in the United States' democracy.

Systemic racism also manifested itself in George Floyd's murder. Many improvements have been made in black communities, but a lot of work is yet to be done. The wanton police murders of black people is a direct outcome of centuries of institutional racism. It is difficult for the United States to hold out itself as a champion of democracy with that banner in one hand and the more than a thousand police killings in the other. It looks hypocritical, to say the least.

What stands out in these two cataclysmic events is President Trump's inability to step forward, take control, and lead from the front. The world looked to the United States for leadership. Most people around the world anticipated the United States' leadership in controlling the coronavirus pandemic. Many countries hoped that the United States would crush the disease and be in a position to help them too. Instead, the world's citizens now gaze with mouths agape as the sole superpower, the most powerful economy on earth, lags behind lesser countries in the race to control the coronavirus pandemic. It is amazing what political ignorance at the head of a great nation can do. It obliterates the adjective *great* completely.

The president, who boasts that he alone can solve the nation's problems, has not to date offered a national strategy. He appears totally incapable of objectively setting out a set of parameters and following them to a logical end. Nine months into the coronavirus pandemic, and the president has not offered a cohesive plan that the nation could rally around. The president appears to be caught up in a dream where his economy was doing extremely well. In that dream, the coronavirus pandemic came and destroyed his economy. He is now awake, but he refuses to acknowledge the coronavirus pandemic as a reality. Like a child, he is laser focused on his toy, this great economy. Nothing else in the world matters but its restoration.

President Trump is incorrigible. It is difficult to imagine that those around him have not made suggestions that he should step out and project himself as a world-class leader. Members of this group must have given him a few tips on how he should go about this. This has to be what happened, but he ignored all recommendations and advice and is bent on doing what he alone knows how to do. A possible alternative explanation is that those around him are scared stiff to offer recommendations that do no emanate from the president's own infertile brain.

It is unfathomable to contemplate a United States president who is not able to get anything right. It is also unimaginable that a United States president seeks to divide the nation every step of the way. President Trump is supposed to be this master builder, but it would appear that his favorite tool is one that was abandoned more than fifty years ago—the wrecking ball. On the political, economic, and social construction site, President Trump is destroying everything with his wrecking ball. It is very hard to find one instance in his first term in office where he could be classified as a unifying force.

President Trump carries his ancient wrecking ball with him on his international diplomatic missions as well. As a builder, he seems to have no interest in the standing foundation. He has to demolish the existing structure and build it from scratch. The North American Free Trade Agreement is gone, and a new edifice is constructed with the Trump brand stamped on it. The ravages of the wrecking ball are all over the Paris Climate Agreement and the Trans Pacific Partnership. The World Health Organization, the United Nations, and the North Atlantic Treaty Organization got hit too, but they did not crumble. There has to be something in that mentality that cannot appreciate the good in a standing edifice. All of President Obama's policies faced the ancient wrecking ball. Few have survived, and the Affordable Care Act is gravely damaged.

It is clear that the president does not know that the Constitution gives him the power to take control and fix national problems. He does not seem to know that the early United States (1776–1787) did not have a president and ran into national crises that it could not resolve. Furthermore, he does not know that the framers created his office to be in charge of all the states in a crisis. Granted that all these scenarios are true, the Centers for Disease Control (CDC) is an agency of the executive branch of the government and is under the president's authority. The president could simply sit back and let the CDC do its work undisturbed. However, even this mundane task is above the president's grasp. Instead, he gets in the way of the CDC and tweets derogatory remarks about its members while they are before the nation, trying to help it to control the coronavirus pandemic.

President Trump has had innumerable opportunities to connect with the American people, but he has missed all of them. The insane genius that he is, he can't realize that all he has to do is level with the American people and assure them that he knows what he is doing.

Many ordinary Americans, politicians or lay people, would be able to say, "Fellow Americans, we are facing a dangerous invisible enemy. We have to fight it together. The CDC has discovered that washing hands frequently, respecting social distancing (six feet apart), and wearing a mask will help us to control the disease until a vaccine or a cure can be found. Work with me, and I promise you that we will get through this together. I am depending on all Americans to help me win the war against this invisible enemy. Thank you and God bless America!"

This very simple statement, said in humility and sounding genuine, would be a beginning. However, the nation gets nothing like this from the president. First he denied the coming of the coronavirus and deemed it a Democratic hoax. He falsely assured the people that the disease would disappear in the summer. No matter how high the number of infection grows or how high the death rate, the president still insists that the coronavirus pandemic is under control. The president recommends taking drugs that the FDA and other medical authorities find to be dangerous and that cannot expel the disease. President Trump even recommends injecting disinfectants in people's bodies to knock out the disease. Only an insane genius is capable of this level of thinking.

President Trump recommending the injection of
disinfectants to eliminate the coronavirus disease

With his economy stuck in his head, he pushes the states to reopen their economies in violation of his own CDC guidelines. He is guilty of facilitating the spiking of the disease. He wants school to reopen while the coronavirus is reaching record levels each day. The difference between the coronavirus and a category five hurricane is the noise. The coronavirus is far quieter than a hurricane, but it is far more deadly. Sending the students, teachers, and support staff back into the classrooms is like sending them out into a raging category five hurricane. The building may be sturdy and can withstand the hurricane's fury, but nothing so far has been able to slow the coronavirus onslaught when people are clustered.

President Trump failed to show leadership in the George Floyd murder as well. The opportunities to take control were as numerous as those offered by the coronavirus pandemic. The president casually mentioned that he saw the murder on television and that it was awful. He later offered to issue an executive order that bore no resemblance to the demands the people in the Black Lives Matter marches were asking for. A single television appearance in which the president calls on the nation to come together and work to end police brutality would have placed him in the realm of leaders. Instead, every action the president took intensified the fury of the marchers in the streets. Calling out the guards to tear-gas the marchers was the worst thing President Trump could have done. He never once tried to deescalate the crisis. He did everything to divide the people.

12

FEDERALISM IN CRISIS SITUATIONS

President Trump got it right when he declared that the coronavirus disease was an invisible enemy and that the United States was at war. As commander in chief of the armed forces, his duties appear to have ended with the pronouncement that the United States was at war. Prior to that pronouncement, the president had made the most serious blunder in war. The commander in chief underestimated the enemy. He described the enemy as a Democratic hoax and predicted that it would surrender without a pitched battle. This was the worst assessment a commander in chief could make when the enemy is threatening invasion of American soil. The enemy spies had already penetrated Washington State and likely had infiltrated other states as well.

This was not a war that involved the superior military arsenal that President Trump so often brags about. This was an invisible enemy that the president's new seventeen-thousand-miles-per-hour weapon was impotent against. What the commander in chief needed to do was put his creative skills on display to save the nation he swore to protect. He failed miserably. The Centers for Disease Control (CDC) in this particular war was the War Room. It was slow in getting its act together, but it did eventually come up with an evidence-based strategy that could work. For the strategy to work, the commander in chief had to embrace all the guidelines of the CDC. The commander in chief failed again. He has never fully focused on the invisible enemy.

His greatest economy on earth was always his center of focus. This is another monumental blunder in war. The commander in chief cannot afford any form of distraction when he is facing a war that involves the health of the people and security of the United States.

An objective analysis of the coronavirus pandemic war would reveal that the United States was in a very unique situation. It was not the first nation to be invaded by the coronavirus disease. The intelligence services and the journalists had an obligation to do more than just reporting. They should have both hit the panic button because they had a better close-up view than all other Americans. The United States Congress should have been in a position to respond in a minute's notice. Congress's failure is most egregious because members knew President Trump's limitation. The collectivity of Congress's power is awesome. Congress should have put in place its own contingency plans and prepared to use its override powers in the event that the president got in the way. Congress has not yet formulated a plan. The president has not prepared a national plan either. These are national failures of inestimable proportions.

Federalism is in desperate trouble here. Some historical comparisons are appropriate in this state of confusion. The nation has faced calamities before, and current leaders can draw from the examples of former leaders. When the Civil War erupted in 1861, President Lincoln's leadership was exemplary. He rallied the nation and awakened all its latent potentials, won the war, and reunited the nation—a feat seldom achieved in the annals of history.

President Franklin D. Roosevelt came to the office with the nation reeling from the effects of the Great Depression. President Roosevelt was resolute about what he wanted to do to heal the nation. He pushed through his New Deal initiatives in the face of fierce opposition, but he was never dissuaded. He was ahead of his time, and he led his people from the front. When World War II broke out, President Roosevelt transitioned to another level of leadership and handed the United States people and the world a victory over the enemies of democracy. President Truman learned his lessons well at the feet of Franklin D.

Roosevelt. He brought the war with Japan to an abrupt end. History may challenge his strategies, but leaders have critical decisions to make in times of crisis. President Truman made his decision with the lives of Americans foremost in his mind.

In 1962, the world stopped breathing as the two superpowers, the Soviet Union and the United States, confronted each other over what has become known as the Cuban Missile Crisis. The Soviet Union had planted missiles in Cuba, all pointing toward the United States, just ninety miles away. President John F. Kennedy led from the front. First, he blockaded the island of Cuba. The Cuban blockade was a resolute move. Great leaders do not vacillate. Over a thirteen-day period, the Soviet Union assessed the situation and decided to dismantle the missiles. President Kennedy, for his part, promised not to invade Cuba. A resuscitated world breathed again.

Today's leaders have all these leadership examples in crisis situations. However, partisan politics has drained the nation's leaders of the capacity to put the American people above all other considerations. The coronavirus pandemic demands that partisan politics be abandoned in the interest of the American people. President Trump has the power vested in him by the Constitution to convene Congress and stress that the exigency of the times demand that the nation moves together as a solid unit. He has the power to demand that Congress supports him in the national interest. No congressperson would want to be an outlier in the fight against the deadly coronavirus pandemic. However, the president allows all this available opportunity to pass him by, as he is singularly focused on his greatest economy and his reelection.

This is the most powerful economy on earth is the boast in all corners. People locally and all over the world heard this refrain so often that they have all come to believe it. The coronavirus pandemic has blown away the façade, and now observers can make their own assessments using the new available evidence.

The following realities seem to suggest that the criteria used to determine the greatest economy on earth have been flawed. For one thing, the greatest economy on earth should not have over 20 percent of its work force joining food lines within a week of the coronavirus pandemic shutdown. More than 13 percent of the nation's population should not have been filing for unemployment within three weeks of the shutdown. Homeowners should not be facing foreclosure in the first months of the coronavirus manifestation; nor should tenants be facing evictions. Blacks and minority groups should not have been disproportionately infected and killed by the coronavirus disease.

Moreover, the greatest economy on earth would have assessed the situation and put measures in place to flatten the curve and keep the infestation rate down. The fact that Taiwan, New Zealand, South Korea, Cuba, Canada, and most of the countries in the European Union have flattened the curve while the United States is still spiking speaks volume about the greatest economy on earth. To date, more than eight million Americans have been infected with the coronavirus disease, and more than 220, 000 have died. The coronavirus pandemic does more than maim and kill; it also exposes the truth. If an economy does not work for all the people, the nation does not have the right to claim the title of the greatest economy in the world.

The following paragraphs will attempt to explain what the coronavirus pandemic suggests that the solutions should have been. The findings should also be recommended as a possible solution template for future health crises of the magnitude of the coronavirus pandemic. To begin with, federalism, with its fifty states working individually to control and eradicate the coronavirus disease, is patently impractical. To add to this confusion, there are more than three thousands counties and boroughs within the fifty states, each with some degree of autonomy. This is a recipe for failure. What is needed is a national plan.

The same day President Trump informed the nation that the United States was at war with an invisible enemy, he should have announced the plan of action that the nation would follow. If a plan was not ready, he should have announced an estimated date when it would be ready. To date, that plan has not materialized. President Trump has the unenviable responsibility of putting a plan together to control and end the coronavirus pandemic now and for the future; that is what the

American people elected him to do. So far, he does not seem to have a clue how to go about this. From a layman's perspective, this is what a national plan of action to fight the coronavirus pandemic should look like.

Constitutionally, only Congress can declare war. As this is a war situation, the president should implore Congress to declare war on the coronavirus pandemic. In a war, the president as the commander in chief relies on his generals and the armed forces to direct operations. If Congress refuses to declare war, the president has a second option. The military has a limited role in the domestic affairs of the United States, but it has been called out by various presidents to maintain law and order and to enforce the desegregation of public school in the 1950s and early 1960s. The coronavirus pandemic qualifies as a special circumstance, and therefore the president can authorize the use of the military in arguably the greatest domestic threat the nation has ever faced. In this special circumstance, the United States is not depending on the military's weaponry. It is the discipline and the trained capabilities of the military that would make a difference if deployed throughout the United States to fight the coronavirus disease. The military and civilian personnel would have to work together in this war.

A Recommended National Plan of Action for Current and Future Pandemics

- As a first step, the president must call on the private sector, the military, academia, Congress (bipartisan group), and individuals to all come up with possible plans of action. They should have a maximum of seven days to do this.
- The president must then establish a task force to examine all the plans and probably adapt the best one or use elements of all to put a best-possibility plan together.

- This final plan will become the blueprint for the present war on the coronavirus pandemic and future health crises, subject to modifications engendered on the battlefield.
- Next, the plan must incorporate the CDC's evidence-based guidelines—frequent hand washing, social distancing, and wearing a mask in public and when social distancing is not possible. The plan must have some result-based timeline before any changes are forthcoming.
- Next, the president must explicitly outline the role of the military in the coronavirus pandemic war. The generals will supervise the enforcement of the president's plan of action.
- The military draft should be reinstituted for the duration of the war on the coronavirus pandemic. All people between eighteen and forty years of age would be on call. Military training would begin forthwith. The goal of this move would be twofold; the creation of pandemic heroes and the reduction of unemployment to zero. As a reward, all participants would have future education paid for by the federal government.
- The president must solicit the help of the military medical personnel who possess the discipline for all situations. They are also going to help with the formation and enforcement of the nationwide plan of action.
- The president must then supervise the implementation of the plan.
- The president must formulate a national plan of suppression. The president has the power to suspend some individual rights in the interest of the public good. He also has the power to deploy the military and call up the National Guard and the Army Corps of Engineers in this unique circumstance.
- Once the plan is adapted, the first step is to implement it nationwide. The national plan of action will subsume all local and state initiatives.
- A special team of managers recruited from the private and public sectors and assisted by military personnel should be put

in place to coordinate the entire national project and report to the president on a daily basis.

- State governors must follow the national plan of action under the president's command in the coronavirus war. Other state duties will go on as usual.
- The president must issue a forty-five-day stay-at-home order, under national supervision.
- Serious penalties must be in place for those who violate the rules, which should include a limit on all gatherings to no more than ten persons.
- Nationwide curfews must be a feature of the plan.
- The president must invoke the Defense Production Act and keep it functional until the goals of the plan are achieved. Just as citizens have to give up their individual rights to make the plan work, American industries must forego some of their profit-making ventures in the interest of the nation's good health. This is also germane to the industries' well-being. Industries need a healthy workforce to produce at the highest levels.
- American industries will produce all the necessary health care supplies.
- People who work in the essential services should be the only ones on the streets.
- Schools, churches, camps, parks, and other venues where people cluster must be on the forty-five-day lockdown, at a minimum. Reopening must be contingent upon the success of the plan.
- National test teams must be trained and deployed to every corner of the United States and the commonwealth.
- The president must invoke the services of all private and public laboratories. Some will focus on research, while others must be upgraded to help to create rapid return on tests to facilitate isolation, quarantine, and contact tracing.
- A whole fleet of contract tracing personnel must be trained and deployed nationwide.

- The president must establish the infrastructure to deliver medical supplies, food, and all other necessities throughout the United States and the commonwealth.
- A feature of the plan of action must be the implementation and enforcement of a national health card system. If the individual does not have a health care plan, the card will indicate that information. If there is a health care plan, it is recorded on the card.
- The plan should mandate that in the future, all citizens must have a health care plan and a health card.
- The president must challenge the technology community to come up with a template for this card. Eventually, the United States will develop the capacity to identify every American's health care status. Health care is a right, and this card will help to move the nation toward providing health care for everyone.
- Future crises should not repeat the ravages of the coronavirus pandemic.
- When the curve is flattened, the Defense Production Act can be suspended, with the understanding that the president has snap back power should the necessity warrant it.
- When the curve is flattened, the commander in chief can suspend the deployment of military personnel.
- All other segments of the plan will be scaled down, premised on its success.
- All elements of the plan must be on standby until a cure or a vaccine is discovered and distributed nationwide.
- The nation must be educated on the efficacy of all citizens getting the vaccine if and when is one is developed.
- The president must be ready to snap back all elements of the plan if the necessity warrants it.
- The president's plan of action must be on standby and high alert as the annual flu season approaches.

Even if the plan did not have the intended results, the American people would be able to hold their heads high, for the leadership would have been assessed as having put out a gallant effort. They would be proud of their leadership and be willing to go back to the drawing board in an effort to find other solution strategies. As it stands at the moment, however, the United States looks weak because some segments of the leadership structure are prepared to allow disparities and inequities so long as their nests are feathered. Many of them are not alarmed at the current situation. They are prepared to go back to business as usual, disregarding all the warning signals coming from the coronavirus pandemic and the Black Lives Matter marches. They are, however, in for a rude awakening. This is the United States' opportunity to do some very serious evaluation. No matter how one assesses the developments over the past nine months, one thing is certain: the nation cannot return to the policies that brought it to the existing crisis.

President Trump does not like testing because it shows the frightening numbers of Americans infected by the coronavirus pandemic. He hates the coronavirus pandemic more because it slows down his greatest economy and shows his lack of leadership. The leadership of the country has to take responsibility for the devastation of the minority communities because for decades nothing was done to prepare the nation for contingencies like the coronavirus pandemic. Nor was anything done to address the pervasive systemic racism that drives policy-making decisions.

The people on the streets have spoken, and they want change. It is disturbing to watch the members of the House and the Senate still engaged in their lofty, standoffish posture. Senators are displaying their usual arrogance. They have not heard the people on the streets, and the coronavirus pandemic did not hit them in the pocket, so they are unmoved. The people on the streets and the coronavirus pandemic have just reminded them that they have been receiving their paychecks under false pretenses, but they have not grasped that either. There is still talk about liberal and ultraliberals, but the American people do not care if it is the conservatives or ultraconservatives who deliver, so long as the government begins to deliver. The people have called for better behavior from the law enforcement establishment. They have called for an end to systemic racism. They want the inequities in society to end. They are calling for transparency and accountability. What the people want is all that matters. They have spoken and are not prepared to return to normal, for that was very bad for them.

13
SUMMARY

In the United States, the struggle for equality and equal protection under law continues for some segments of the population. Blacks and minorities have seen some progress, but recent events highlight the reality that there is still a long way to go. The collision of the two cataclysmic events, the coronavirus pandemic and the brutal, daylight killing of George Floyd on the street in Minneapolis, places the national focus on the disaffection of minority groups in American society. The nationwide prolonged marches portend a racial reckoning in the United States. The marches have also begun to remind Americans that power in the United States emanates from the people. There are already responses to the protests in the streets as the mayors in several cities and the United States Congress are moving to address the age long police abuse of blacks in the United States.

The coronavirus pandemic has exposed the United States in a variety of ways. The United States' economic power is unquestionable. What is questionable is the use of the United States' economic proceeds. It reminds the nation that there is a deep, underlying unfairness in the United States' economic system. The system was built on the backs of blacks who were never compensated. It is never too late for showers of reparation.

Two hundred and thirty years later, blacks were directly in the path of the coronavirus pandemic, as they were found to be without adequate health care, underpaid or unemployed, and living in substandard neighborhoods. The coronavirus disease disproportionately maimed and killed them. Representative John Lewis, "the conscience of Congress," did his best to redress the situation, but now that he is gone, his surviving colleagues owe him a debt of gratitude. They must pick up where he left off and address the issue of black and minority economic and social inequities. Their right to vote must not be tampered with.

Donald Trump, the candidate in the 2016 presidential campaign, has significantly tarnished the United States' political image. High school, college, and university students who learned debating strategies must have been mortified during the 2016 presidential campaign. All the debate formalities they learned were crushed and replaced with a level of crudity that does not belong in the most advanced economy in the world. To denigrate the group of people contending with you for an office shows a total lack of respect for that office. It also displays a lack of self-respect. Additionally, it shows a lack of respect for the electorate that candidate Trump was trying to win over. Moreover, it is simply an undemocratic behavior. The group is vying for the same office. Members usually have more similarities than they have differences. To call each other names that would be regarded as an assault on the individual in normal circumstances is sinking to the lowest denominator in electioneering.

This damage can be repaired easily. All it takes is for future candidates to pledge not to indulge in anything that resembles the Trump approach in campaigning. It is appropriate for candidates to follow normal protocols and address opponents with respect and dignity. By advancing clear and convincing evidence that candidates know what they are talking about and that they believe in the ideology and the policies they are promoting are electioneering best practices. A presidential campaign should appeal to the electorates' highest instincts and ideals and raise their expectations to lofty heights. The days, weeks, and months ahead will give the electorate time to reflect on who the candidate is and what their words mean.

When the candidate speaks in these terms, the electorate feels respected and begins the process of assessing the various candidates who come seeking their support. This method is likely to earn the candidate a broad swath of the voting population. People at all levels of the society will evaluate the candidate by their words, tone, and methods of articulation. If the candidate is ruckus and rowdy, they are likely to win over the ruckus and the rowdy type. If these types are the dominant population, the candidate's chances of winning are high. However, if there is a broad mix of electorates, then the more polished the candidate's delivery, the higher the chances of winning a cross section of the population.

On the other hand, President Trump's display of ignorance during the campaign and throughout his presidency will be much harder to repair. Some of the damages that President Trump caused to the Constitution may be irreparable. For example, an inevitable battle must be waged to amend the Constitution so that future presidents cannot use the pardon for the benefit of friends and associates. President Trump blatantly used the pardon for these reasons. It is an assault on the justice system and a violation of the rule of law. If this practice is not addressed immediately, future friends of the president will commit all manner of atrocities and demand presidential pardons.

When the framers of the Constitution conceptualized the pardon, the United States was basically an agricultural society, with people living in small towns where everyone knew everyone else, or they lived in small rural communities. Today, in a high-technology information age, conditions are quite different. Some cities have populations of tens of millions, and the president could be an individual of shady character and unscrupulous business practices. The pardon today could have all sorts of negative implications. If Congress and the states fail to initiate this amendment, it could signify a nail in the Constitution's coffin.

The United States Constitution, with all its cracks that occurred during the long and arduous process of molding it and those that have developed over the 233 years of its existence, has served the nation well. The Trump presidency has brought the cracks into sharper focus than any other presidency. This is partly because no other president has been so uninformed about the Constitution's content. Moreover, no previous president has been as contemptuous and disrespectful of the document.

Already President Trump's supporters in the Republican Party have done away with the framers' concept that foreign state actors interfering in the United States' domestic politics is impermissible. In the 2016 presidential election, Russia interfered in the United States' presidential election in order to help the Republican candidate Donald Trump win. The Department of Justice established a special counsel to investigate Russia's interference in the 2016 presidential election. Attorney General William Barr horridly wrote a summary of the report without reading the full report, in order to give President Trump a false cover that the Mueller Report found no collusion with Russia.

The United States Congress and the United States people have yet to see the full report. President Trump has blocked all of the House of Representatives' efforts to get hold of those documents and to have President Trump's aides testify before that august body. Under President Trump, the House of Representatives' oversight powers are greatly diminished. Those aides who did their duties in defiance of President Trump's orders were summarily fired after the Senate exonerated him in the impeachment trial.

The damages done to the checks and balances functions of Congress will be difficult to repair. If this element of the Constitution continues to be eroded, the survival of the document will be placed in jeopardy. President Trump's disdain for the House of Representatives, which is controlled by the opposition Democratic Party, is legendary. As he did when he was candidate for the presidency, he selects the most denigrating terms to describe members of that party and particularly the Speaker of the House. President Trump slaughtered House decorum once he lost the House of Representatives in the midterm election of 2018.

More importantly, American citizens should regard President Donald Trump's abuse of power as setting many precedents. It has been documented that this president is politically ignorant and very self-centered. He really makes a great deal of bluster, but he is not a high-level thinker. Just imagine a future United States president who is really smart and wants to expand on President Trump's erosion of the rule of law and disregard for the checks and balances features of the Constitution. It would require a supreme bipartisan effort to keep him in check.

A Congress such as the one sitting now would witness the transition to authoritarian rule before their very eyes. In his first term, President Donald Trump has wreaked a great deal of havoc with the powers that the Constitution confers on him. He has also encroached on other powers that do not fall under his purview. For example, from time to time, he assumes powers that are strictly reserved to the states. Moreover, he has threatened to cut off funding to the states if they do not fully reopen schools in the fall, even though states are 90 percent self-sufficient in their education funding. He has even ventured into unchartered waters to claim absolute immunity from investigation while he is in office. The Supreme Court in a seven-to-two ruling corrected and reminded him that no one is above the law.

Americans have been subjected to a four-year term of tyranny by the most politically ignorant president to hold that high office. The United States Congress facilitated his tyrannical rule by relinquishing its coequal status and allowing the president to run amok. This is not what the framers of the Constitution expected. Congresspersons have become self-centered, focusing more on their political future than on the nation's interests and needs. However, all is not lost. The marches on the streets of the United States in protest of George Floyd's murder hold out a great deal of hope. The young people on the streets are calling for justice and seem ready to become the change they are calling for.

The coronavirus pandemic has lifted the veil of hypocrisy that shrouded the nation's political, economic, and social accomplishments, and what it reveals is very unpleasant. Changes are going to have to address all the shortcomings. The old methodologies will have to be abandoned. In this technological and information age, the nation's leaders are going to have to come up with policies that address the needs of all the people and not some of the people, as the coronavirus pandemic revealed. In the richest nation on earth, steps must be taken to make sure that the nation's resources are more equitably distributed.

References

Bachrach, P. *Political Elites in a Democracy*. New Brunswick, NJ: Transaction Publishers, 2010.

Brubaker, D. L. *Creative Curriculum Leadership*. 1st ed. Thousand Oaks: California, 1994.

Dahl, R.A. *Who Governs? Democracy and Power in an American City*. Fredericksburg, VA: Bookcrafters, Inc., 1989.

Edwards III, G.C., M.P. Wattenberg, and R.L. Lineberry. *Government in America: People, Politics, and Policy*. 16th ed. Glenview, IL: Pearson Education, Inc., 2014.

Ginsberg, B., T. J. Lowi, and M. Weir. *We the People: An Introduction to American Politics*. 8th ed. New York: W. W. Norton and Company, 2011.

Maidment, R. & Zvesper, J. (1989). *Reflections on the Constitution*. Manchester, England & New York: Manchester University Press.

Mankiw, N. G. (2004). *Principles of Microeconomics* (3rd Edition). Harvard University Press.

Murdock, S. (2016). "U.S. shooting since 1963 have killed more Americans than all wars." Huffington Post

Newman, W. R. (1986). *The Paradox of Mass Politics: Knowledge and Opinion in the American Electorate.* Harvard University Press.

Patel, E. (2012) *Sacred Ground Pluralism, Prejudice, and the Promise of America.* Boston, MA: Unitarian Universalist Association of Congregations.

Yukl, G. (1998). *Leadership in Organizations* (4th Edition). State University of New York at Albany. Prentice Hall, Upper Saddle River, New Jersey07458

About the Author

Winston Sheekel Marsh grew up as a British colonist in Jamaica before the island negotiated its independence on August 6, 1962. He was an educator in the Jamaican school system more than twenty-seven years and has always been an avid student of American history. He is a resident and citizen of the United States of America, where he has taught in colleges and high schools. He is married with six children.

Index

H

healthcare 35, 39, 41, 65, 66, 70, 93,
    106, 107, 110
hegemon 11
Helsinki 25, 94
hoax 36, 98, 100
House of Representatives 23, 25,
    27, 113

I

ideology 21, 111
ignorance 3, 5, 6, 7, 9, 11, 12, 13, 18,
    23, 24, 28, 30, 31, 32, 36, 38, 49,
    52, 54, 57, 58, 61, 67, 72, 79, 80,
    87, 90, 91, 94, 96, 112
immigrants 7, 8, 9
impartial 26, 83, 92
impeachment 23, 26, 27, 36, 92,
    93, 113
inequities 32, 39, 41, 48, 55, 59, 88,
    108, 109, 111
inferiority complex 34
insane genius 7, 9, 11, 73, 75, 81, 91,
    97, 98
inspectors general 92
institutional racism 95
international diplomacy 29, 94
international law 25, 94

J

Jackson, Andrew 76
Jamestown, Virginia 44, 61
jazz 58
Jefferson, Thomas 52, 53, 68
Jim Crow laws 72, 74, 86

K

Kennedy, John F. 17, 102

King, Rev. Dr. Martin Luther, Jr. 48,
    55, 56, 72
Kuwait 15

L

law enforcement 45, 50, 56, 70, 74,
    86, 109
leadership 3, 14, 16, 33, 39, 62, 81, 89,
    91, 96, 99, 101, 102, 108
Lewis, John 75, 111
Lincoln, Abraham 101
literacy test 86
lobbyists 89
lynching 50, 74, 76, 86

M

Madison, James 77, 93
Minneapolis 1, 47, 59, 83, 95, 110
minorities 2, 11, 26, 55, 56, 60, 61, 63,
    69, 72, 95, 110
mothers 49, 50, 51, 52, 74, 75
Mount Rushmore 73, 75
musicians 49, 57

N

National Guard 38, 80, 105
National Rifle Association 77
Native Americans 63, 76
Neumann, Russell 5, 6, 11
New Zealand 103
North American Free Trade
    Agreement 15, 97
North Atlantic Treaty Organization
    15, 97
nuclear arsenal 21

Lightning Source UK Ltd.
Milton Keynes UK
UKHW011845131220
375014UK00010B/758/J